Praise ,

The Pizza Delivery Millionaire

"*The Pizza Delivery Millionaire* is a must read for anyone who ever wanted to invest in real estate but didn't know how to get started. By telling the story of an aspiring real estate investor of modest means, Mr. Vazquez shares the keys to successful real estate investing in a fun and entertaining manner. The book is full of practical recommendations for identifying properties, finding tenants, and most importantly, making money in real estate!"

Jeff Persinger, President BioPharm Communications

"I loved it ! What a great story, now I am ready to invest!"

Norbert Cardenas, Home Inspector, NPS

"*The Pizza Delivery Millionaire* puts everything in a realistic perspective. I can relate to the story, and as a result, I feel confident in taking that next step to finally getting started in real estate investing."

Andre' Lacroix, Volunteer Firefighter

"*The Pizza Delivery Millionaire* is an empowering book that is also so much fun to read! There are simplistic, yet powerful principles woven into a wonderful story of family and friends inspiring the reader throughout the book. Rick reveals a step by step pathway for integrating the essence of real estate investment that is both respectful and wise. This book is filled with ideas that will enhance the journey to the financial freedom each of us deserves.

Suzanne M Spanton, Educational Consultant

I only wish I had *The Pizza Delivery Millionaire* available to me when I started investing. I wouldn't have been as intimidated and would probably have double the portfolio I have now. Thank you, Rick!"

Mike Fuccile, Real Estate Entrepreneur

The Pizza Delivery **Millionaire**

A Layman's Guide to Becoming Financially Free in Real Estate

Rick Vazquez

MJ

New York

™ Pizza Delivery
Millionaire

A Layman's Guide to Becoming Financially Free in Real Estate

by **Rick Vazquez**

© 2007 Rick Vazquez. All rights reserved.

ISBN 978-1-60037-318-3 (Paperback)
ISBN 978-1-60037-319-0 (Hardcover)

Published by:

M O R G A N · J A M E S ™
THE ENTREPRENEURIAL PUBLISHER
www.morganjamespublishing.com

Habitat for Humanity®
Peninsula
Building Partner

Part of the Mega Book Series

Morgan James Publishing, LLC
1225 Franklin Ave. Ste 325
Garden City, NY 11530-1693
Toll Free 800-485-4943
www.MorganJamesPublishing.com

Cover and Interior Design and Layout by:
Bonnie Bushman
bbushman@bresnan.net

Dedication

In memory of my Pop who taught me so many lessons about winning in athletics and winning in the game of life.

Acknowledgments

I would first like to thank my wife Lori for all her love and support over the past eighteen years we have been together. Whether at work, home, or parenting, you have always been by my side encouraging me and supporting me in each and every endeavor along the way.

I would also like to recognize my two children Jordan and Ryan, who constantly make me proud each day to be a Dad and give me the energy and mind-set to realize that having fun each day and giving them unconditional love is more important than anything else.

I want to thank my brother Rob, my Dad and many of my friends and family who have taken the time to listen to me and give advice regarding the idea to write the book and it's content.

I would like to thank David Hancock and Morgan James Publishing for believing in the book and taking a chance on it when nobody else would.

I also want to thank my editors Judy Reynolds and Patricia Ross, for the countless hours they worked on the book to ensure it was professional. They made me look like a real pro.

Special thanks to David Domanski for designing our website and John Morales for producing the audio book.

Finally, I want to thank my Mom, who has always been my biggest fan, supporter and promoter. For the times when life didn't always deal us a fair shake, your perseverance, determination and never-quit attitude helped me become the man I am today.

Table of Contents

Introduction

This book was written in an effort to help the everyday person make it in today's real estate market. Drawing from my experience and the many lessons I have learned along the way, I have condensed all these lessons into this book in an entertaining story format. You will find the book fun to read and easy to understand.

This story is about a pizza delivery driver who lives in Beach, New Jersey, and learns many valuable lessons about financial freedom in his quest to find a career for his future and his financial independence. The book demonstrates specific strategies and tactics to implement in helping a person become a millionaire in today's real estate market. Although the book uses a pizza delivery driver as its main character, he is a metaphor for individuals in any line of business. Whether you are a teacher, police officer, electrician, butcher, or office manager, you can become financially free in real estate.

Many people think that real estate investing is only for the rich, but this book will help to explain how it can be for everyone.

Chapter 1
Looking For A Millionaire

It was just another windy summer day in Beach, New Jersey, a small island off the coast of Atlantic City. Beach was not famous for much; however, it was known as the windiest city in the United States. Many of the town's residents became familiar with this piece of trivia after it was published in the local paper that "Beach, New Jersey" was the answer to a trivia question on "Jeopardy" almost six years ago.

Beach was a small shore town without the nuances of the crazy vacation town traffic and atmosphere. Most of the people in town were either employed by the casinos or worked in the blue collar world as electricians, butchers, store owners, teachers and other jobs that kept the town running smoothly.

"Ryan Reynolds, are you ready for another busy day of delivering pizzas?" asked Jimmy McHugh, one of the two Irish brothers who owned *Two Brothers Pizza* on the corner of thirtieth and thirty first streets.

"I am as ready as ever. I hope today is a busy day. I am trying to save for my Mom and Pop's birthday which is coming up in July," answered Ryan.

"Well, you know the heavy season doesn't start until July fourth weekend but business usually picks up in the last week of June," explained Jimmy.

"What is your schedule like today Ryan, is it another jam-packed day?"

"Yes it is, and I wouldn't have it any other way," exclaimed Ryan.

"I worked at the tennis shack from seven to ten this morning and then ran the recreation programs from ten to twelve and here I am for another double shift until eleven."

"Well at least you are not working the bar and grill after today's shift like you did yesterday," said Jimmy.

"That's true, the bar and grill is not usually crowded tonight so there is no need for me to go in."

"Don't you ever get tired of working all those jobs?" asked Jimmy.

"Not really. Sometimes if I am at the bar and grill late, it gets tough, but I enjoy all the jobs I am doing. I work at the tennis shack because the hours are early, and it is great exercise in the morning. I work for the recreation department because I like helping out the kids, and I enjoy seeing their smiling faces each day. I work here because after your brother beat me playing tennis he felt bad for me and felt he had to make it up to me and offered me a job delivering pizza," laughed Ryan.

"How about the bar and grill?" Jimmy asked.

"I work there because my brother and a few of my friends work there. What is better than hanging out with your friends and getting paid for it?" answered Ryan.

"I know you enjoy all these jobs but do you ever think about what you want to do for a career or with your future?" questioned Jimmy.

"To be honest I never really think about it. I am sure one day I will wake up and say, 'I think I am going to be a doctor, lawyer or maybe a fireman,'" responded Ryan.

"Maybe you'll become a third partner in a pizza place I know in town," joked Jimmy.

"Maybe," said Ryan. "How would you change the sign out there? Two Brothers and a Delivery guy Pizza Shop?" Both men laughed as Jimmy went into the back to get the dough ready for the day's orders.

For the first time in his life, Ryan really thought about what Jimmy had asked him. What did he want to do with his life? He was sure he couldn't do all four of these jobs forever, and he knew he couldn't live off the salary of any one of them. Plus, he wanted to get married one day and have a family. He really needed to think this over and make a decision.

It was in that moment he decided that he would make this his goal for the summer. By the end of August, he wanted to decide what to do with his life and then take the appropriate actions to make it happen.

That night after work, Ryan went home and went to the backyard to shoot some foul shots. Ryan always shot foul shots when he had a problem that needed a solution or if he really just needed to think. His Pop had taught him that making foul shots is 10% skill and 90% concentration. He always used foul shots as a tool to concentrate and at the same time clear his mind of everything and anything else that was going on in his life.

The other thing Ryan did when he had a problem was go talk to his best friend, his Pop, his grandfather. Pop didn't always give him the answers, but most times with a few hints from Pop, Ryan could draw his own conclusion on what was the best way to handle a given situation.

One of the good things about going to see Pop was that he was a night owl. Therefore, Ryan could go over there late at night without ever worrying if he would wake him. Ryan decided since he really didn't get a good answer for himself after shooting the foul shots he better go to plan B which had worked countless times for him in the past, he headed over to Pop's house.

"Hey Pop, what is going on ?" asked Ryan.

"Same stuff. The Yanks can't win more than two in a row and it's almost Shubie season again," responded Pop.

A Shubie was a term used by the locals for people who came down to the island in the summer either for a weekend or for the entire season. The origin of the name started back when people from New York and Philadelphia would go to the shore for the day and pack their lunch in their shoeboxes. Ever since then, the name stuck and was used frequently in conversation with any locals between July 4th and September 1st.

"How was work today?" asked Pop.

"Well, that is a good question. It was good and bad I guess," answered Ryan. "It was good because it was busy, and I made some good money. But it was bad because Jimmy asked me a question I didn't know the answer to, and I have been thinking about it all day."

"Maybe I can help," said Pop.

"Maybe you can. I am afraid this one is going to be one for me to answer, but I did come here to try to get some help," said Ryan.

"Jimmy asked me, 'what am I going to do with my life and career.' I didn't have an answer for him. Then it started to hit me; I can't work these part time jobs forever and maybe I should start to focus and think long term about what I am going to do for a career."

"Well, as we do most times when we try to solve a problem together, let's start with your goals," Pop said eagerly.

"Well, I guess my goal is like many others in this town or any town for that matter; I want to be a millionaire," answered Ryan.

Pop responded, "Okay, then you need to try to find out how you can become a millionaire. There are many millionaires in the world and many of them became that way in hundreds of different ways. I am sure that there are many millionaires on this island and you don't even know it.

"Try asking people you come in contact with over the next few months what they think and then gather up all the ideas and then sort through them and come up with a plan for yourself."

"Sounds good to me," Ryan said, with a little extra energy in his response.

"Okay, good. Now I am expecting twenty tomorrow night in the game," chuckled pop.

Pop was referring to the basketball league Ryan played in, which was the local men's league with all the guys from the town. Pop still loved to come watch Ryan play, and Ryan enjoyed having him at the games.

On his way home that night, Ryan realized that it turned out to be a good day after all. Although he did not have all the answers to some of these new questions, he did have a plan of action, and he also had some time to put a game plan together. Plus, he worked four part-time jobs, he was bound to come across a few millionaires from time to time. He just had to find a way to know one when he saw one, so he could pick their brain.

Chapter 2
An Unlikely Millionaire

One of the things Ryan learned growing up from Pop was that preparation can equal success. Whether it is sports, school or work, most times preparation starts with organization, and he learned to be good at that.

Ryan always kept a calendar in his car that detailed his work schedule, his game schedule, and leisure activities. Since he was driving around delivering pizzas most of the day, his car seemed like the best place to keep the calendar in case he had to update it from time to time.

However, today he was bringing a notebook to include in his travels. Since he never knew when he was going to meet one of these millionaires, he better be prepared.

Even though he considered himself a very organized person, Ryan didn't consider himself a great note taker. There were a few times in college when he looked back to review some notes he had taken in class and he couldn't even read them. He was not sure if this was because he was not a good note taker or because he was left handed and most times the words were smeared across the page.

On the top of the first page Ryan wrote, "Millionaires." He was not sure what else to put at this time. Ryan was still fuzzy on what he was going to do once he found a millionaire or what he would ask him or her. However, one thing he knew, he was determined to identify some millionaires over the summer and then in turn take some action for his own career.

It was now about 11:50, and he had to be to work in 10 minutes. Ryan put on his red and yellow *Two Brothers Pizza* tee shirt, grabbed his notebook, and jumped into the car. On his way to work he thought about how he would find these millionaires. Then he thought to himself, "I can't just deliver a pizza and say, 'here is your large pie with mushrooms, by the way are you a millionaire'?" He guessed he could look for some hints or signs that someone was a millionaire and maybe then just ask them what they do for a living. His mind was racing a mile a minute and then he realized, he had all summer to find some millionaires, so maybe he didn't need to track them all down on the first day of his quest.

Before Ryan arrived at work, he stopped at the gas station and filled up the car with gas so he wouldn't have to stop during his shift. Plus, Thursdays were usually busy nights so if he was stopping for gas it would take time away from making money delivering.

"Ryan, what's up," asked Brian. Brian was Jimmy McHugh's brother and the other owner of the pizza shop. Thursdays is his day to work.

"Not much, I'm ready for a new quest today," Ryan said enthusiastically.

"Does it involve that notebook in your hand?" asked Brian.

"You could say that," Ryan replied

"It is not going to effect the delivering of our orders today is it?" questioned Brian.

"Never, this is a summer long journey, and today is the first day. This notebook is for the notes I am going to take once I find a few millionaires on this island and ask them how they became rich."

"Please tell me you don't think it is only going to take you writing down a few notes to become a millionaire?" asked Brian. "I am sure becoming a millionaire is hard work."

Ryan responded "I am not saying it is an easy task, but I do think if I can find a few patterns of some millionaires or a particular field they are in, it could help me determine what I want to do with my life."

"As long as it doesn't effect our delivery times," joked Brian.

"It won't," claimed Ryan.

"Maybe *you* can even help me find some of these millionaires on this island. You have had the pizza shop for 15 years; you know about 95% of the people who live here."

"I guess I can try, but to be honest I try not to get involved in people's financial situations. I have heard a few rumors over the years, but I can't confirm any of them for sure," said Brian.

"Well, any help is appreciated," Ryan said with a smile.

The rest of the day Ryan spent looking at all kinds of surroundings around town that he thought could help him identify a few millionaires. He was looking at houses, cars in driveways, and the way people dressed. Although he had a few ideas, he found nothing he felt comfortable asking someone about.

Then about 10:30 pm, Brian gave him an order to the address of 600 Washington Drive. He said to Ryan before he left, "I have heard this guy is a millionaire but don't quote me on that."

"Thanks Brian."

This surprised Ryan because Washington Drive was down by the golf course and was in a section that was known to be the "regular" people of the island. The houses were not that big; they were mostly younger families down there, and it was about 6 blocks from the beach. He thought to himself, "Maybe he won't say anything about being a millionaire, but at least I will get to see where one lives."

When Ryan pulled up to the house it was an average size split level with no garage and a front yard not much bigger than where he lived. Ryan thought to himself, "There is no way this guy can be a millionaire. This house is a little bigger than mine and not nearly the size of what I would expect in the millionaire category." He grabbed the pizza and walked up and knocked on the door.

"Two Brothers Pizza," he yelled.

"One second," a voice responded from the house.

Then the door opened and there in front of him was a man about six feet tall wearing a cut off tee shirt and black mesh shorts.

"Great, I am so hungry," the man said with a smile.

"Your total is $10.60," Ryan answered.

He gave Ryan $14 and told him to keep the change. Ryan thanked him, as he did all his customers, and walked back to the car. He didn't have the nerve to ask him anything about being a millionaire, plus after what he just saw, he would be willing to bet he was not even close to being a millionaire.

He didn't look like a millionaire. His house was not a millionaire's house; his clothes were no different than Ryan's, and the car in driveway was about 10 years old.

As Ryan headed back to the pizza shop he thought that Brian was playing a trick on him. Brian was famous for playing tricks on the employees and Ryan was no exception. Everyone in town wanted to work for Two Brothers Pizza because word had spread that it had a great atmosphere and you could make some decent money while having fun at work. Plus, Ryan was never shy about getting in on the action with regard to the practical jokes, and he thought Brian was just paying him back.

"Well, how did it go?" asked Brian.

Confused by the question, Ryan responded "How did it go? What kind of question is that? You got me good on that one. I thought you were going to try to help me."

"I did try to help you. I gave you what I believed was a millionaire. Isn't that what you were looking for?" Brian answered in a puzzled tone.

"Did you talk to him? Did he give you any tips?"

"First of all I did not talk to him," Ryan exclaimed in an annoyed tone. "Secondly, do you think I didn't know you tried to set me up on that one. There is no way that guy was a millionaire. He looked and dressed like you and I. His car is as old as mine and his house is about 200 square feet bigger than my mom's."

"How do you know for sure?" Brian asked.

"Well, I guess I can't know for sure. But I have seen Donald Trump in Atlantic City about 10 times, and I am not quite ready to put them in the same category," answered Ryan.

"Not every millionaire looks like Trump you know. There are thousands of millionaires in the country and all of them don't walk around with a blue suit and red tie everyday," scoffed Brian.

"That could be true but I am willing to bet that the guy I delivered to tonight is not what I am looking for," said Ryan.

"You young kids think you know everything these days. Are you up for a little wager?" asked Brian.

"You want to make a bet with me that the guy at 600 Washington Drive is a millionaire?" questioned Ryan.

"Yes, are you up for it?"

"I sure am. This looks like the easiest bet I have ever made," claimed Ryan. "What do you want to bet?"

"How about this. If he is a millionaire, you mop the floors at closing time for a week so the girls can go home early, and if you win, I will pay you for two extra full shifts. Does that sound fair?" Brian asked with a big grin on his face.

"Fair, where do I sign?" responded Ryan.

Brian and the employees always had little side wagers going on in the pizza shop. Most of the time they were for either an ice cream cone or for chores around the shop that nobody ever wanted to do.

Brian was also known for not making great bets. Many people thought he lost about 70% of the bets he made with his employees.

Ryan was not sure if his judgment was that bad or if it was just another way to keep the morale high in the pizza shop and the atmosphere light hearted.

"How are we going to find out," Ryan asked.

"I will call him and tell him you are coming," responded Brian.

"What are you going to say? Hey mister, I am sending my delivery driver down to ask you a personal question; can you please answer him honestly?" joked Ryan.

"That is exactly what I am going to say," answered Brian. "Hold on one second, and you can take this other order to Lincoln Drive with you."

It was about this time Ryan thought he was going a little crazy. But he made the deal, and he was about to get paid for two extra shifts, which could help with the extra money he needed for Mom and Pop's birthday presents. As he grabbed the delivery for Lincoln Drive off the counter, he heard Brian on the phone.

"Hey Steve, this is Brian from Two Brothers Pizza. I need a favor. I am sending down one of my delivery drivers to ask you a quick question. Do you think you can be honest with him?"

Although Ryan could not hear the other end of the conversation, it seemed as if Brian got the answer he was looking for.

"Ok Ryan, he is waiting for you," said Brian.

Ryan answered with a half smile, half laugh in his voice. "I'll be back in 10 minutes. Do me a favor, can you please have the money ready for the two extra shifts tonight when I leave so I can get my Pop his birthday present tomorrow?"

Brian answered, "I will do better than that, if you win, I will pay you out by the time you take your next delivery."

"Sounds good to me," Ryan said as he walked out of the shop and shut the door behind him heading for the car.

As he headed back to Washington Drive, Ryan was very confident that he would be taking home some extra pay tonight. He even started thinking about what birthday presents he was going to buy tomorrow. Then it dawned on him: "can I really just ask a stranger if he is a millionaire? What if he jumps down my throat? What if he gets upset and then we lose him as a customer?" Then he thought about it in a little more detail. Brian already called him so he must know some type of tough question is coming.

When Ryan pulled up to the house, it was rather weird. He didn't have a pizza in his hand and he was just strolling up the walkway like he was going to a friend's house. Once again he rang the doorbell and yelled, "Two Brothers Pizza."

The same man answered the door as before. As the door opened Ryan put his hand out to introduce himself. "I am Ryan Reynolds. I work for Brian at the pizza shop."

"Yes, he told me you were coming, and I remember you from before," answered the man. "I am Steve Glass, nice to meet you."

"Sorry to bother you, but Brian and I have a little wager going on and I had to come down to ask you a question to settle it."

"Well I hope I can help. I will try to answer it the best I can," said Steve.

"I will keep it brief, and to be honest if you are not comfortable answering, please feel free to tell me."

It was at this time that Ryan got a big knot in his stomach. He was never shy; he dealt with dozens of customers and kids on a daily basis, so why was he so nervous about asking a simple little question? He decided to just get it out, so he could get this over with.

"Are you a millionaire?" asked Ryan. To Ryan it seemed like it took Steve 45 seconds to answer, but in reality it was probably about 2-3 seconds.

"Actually, yes I am," responded Steve.

"Really!" said Ryan surprisingly.

"Let me guess, were you expecting a Donald Trump type guy?" asked Steve.

"How did you know that?" answered Ryan.

"Everyone in the younger generation thinks that all millionaires look like Trump. They do not yet understand the concept of money and how it works with regard to acquiring wealth. Now it is my turn to ask you a question. Why did you want to know if I was a millionaire?" asked Steve.

"Well, to be honest it is a long story, but the Cliff Notes version is that, basically I am trying to find millionaires on the island this summer. Once I find a few, I am going to ask them a number of questions on how they became millionaires. Then I am going to collect all this data and in turn decide what I want to do for my career."

"That sounds like a good plan," commented Steve. "Count me in."

"Excuse me sir?" responded Ryan surprisingly.

"I said count me in. I am always willing to educate the younger generation in the business world, and maybe we can create a win-win situation here."

Ryan was half-excited and half-puzzled by the response.

"Don't you also work at the tennis shack?" asked Steve.

"Yes I do," said Ryan.

"How about we make a little deal? Every Friday night when you deliver my pizza you bring over three questions you would like answered. Over the weekend I will review the questions then we can play tennis on Monday morning, and I will give you the answers to your questions. It is a win-win situation. I get some exercise and maybe some pointers on the tennis court, and you get answers to your questions for your summer project."

"You got it!" exclaimed Ryan. "Let's make the tennis game for 8:00 am because I teach recreation programs starting at 10:00 am."

"Sounds good to me," answered Steve. Both men shook hands and Ryan headed back to the car.

Although Ryan obviously lost the bet, he was not at all upset. He was so excited that he finally found someone who was a millionaire, and he was even more excited that this millionaire appeared to look like a regular guy. Although there were still a number of mysteries still to be solved, Ryan was well on his way to financial freedom. Then as he drove back to the pizza shop, his mind started racing again. How did he become a millionaire? How long did it take? What would Steve Glass suggest Ryan do to become a millionaire? These three questions and about twenty more filled his head in his 5 minute drive back to *Two Brothers Pizza*. Ryan pulled up in front of the shop, grabbed his notebook and wrote down his first official lesson.

Millionaires Can Look Like You and Me

Chapter 3
Millionaires And Real Estate

The next week, Ryan had to mop the floors each night after work to pay off the bet he lost to Brian. However, he didn't mind because he was getting closer to Friday and his first "official" day to ask Steve questions on how he became a millionaire. During the week, Ryan wrote down about 15 questions he wanted to ask; but he decided to just ask Steve some basic questions, and hopefully Steve would elaborate on the items he felt were most important.

It was about 6:00 pm at the pizza shop when he reminded Brian, "Don't forget. I get the order to Washington Drive for Steve's house."

"I know, I know," said Brian.

Friday night usually was the busiest night of the week, and the pizza shop was jammed. Ryan was taking three and four deliveries at a time, and the next thing he knew it was 9:30. Ryan walked back in from a delivery from the golf course area, and there was a large pie waiting on the counter.

"This is for your boy, Steve," said Brian, "You're up!"

Ryan could not grab the pizza fast enough off the counter and he was on his way. As he drove to the house, he kept saying to himself, "Make sure you ask him smart open ended questions. You don't want him to answer with yes or no answers."

Then Ryan pulled up to the house and grabbed his list of questions. As he walked up to the house, he decided which three questions he would ask Steve for their first session. Then he knocked on the door.

"Steve, good to see you again," Ryan said with a smile.

"Good to see you again Ryan," answered Steve. "Are you all set with your questions?"

"I sure am." "Let's get the pizza business out of the way first," Ryan said eagerly. "That will be $10.60."

"Ryan here is $15. Please keep the change," responded Steve.

"Thanks Steve! Are you ready for my questions?" asked Ryan.

"I think so, unless they are on history or geometry!" Both men laughed.

"I'll start out with some basic ones and hopefully we can build on them," chuckled Ryan. "These are the first three that came to my mind, and my Pop always told me, go with your gut instinct!"

"First, how did you become a millionaire? Second, how long did it take? Third, what would you suggest I do to become a millionaire?"

"These are all very good questions. I should not have a problem answering those on Monday," joked Steve.

"Ok, great," Ryan said. "So I'll see you at 8:00 am on Monday?"

"Yes you will," answered Steve. "Have a good weekend."

"You too," Ryan yelled as he was walking back to the car.

The weekend went by very fast and next thing Ryan knew it was Monday morning. Although he was more of a night owl than an early riser, there were many times when he was still half asleep at at 9:00 am.

However, today was different. He was all pumped up and raring to go at 7:00 am. Then, at about 7:45, he saw Steve walking from his car. As he approached the tennis shack, he looked over at Ryan and asked "Are you ready?"

"I sure am. We are on court #4, which is over here behind the shack," added Ryan.

"I just need to stretch a few minutes, if you don't mind. My body is too old to be jumping right into things. That's how I pulled a hamstring muscle a few weeks back. I still think I am a young gun like you. However, my body keeps reminding me, I'm not."

Ryan chuckled as he responded, "Well the good news for you is that I am not at my best in the mornings."

"Are you ready for my answers?" asked Steve.

"I have been ready since Friday when I delivered your pizza," answered Ryan.

"Okay, first how did I become a millionaire? This is the easiest question of all. I became a millionaire investing in real estate."

"Oh really?" asked Ryan. "Don't you need a lot of money to get into real estate?"

"That is not true Ryan. You do need some money, but we are getting way ahead of ourselves. Let's stick to the basics first and then as our lessons progress, we can get into more details."

"Question #2 was, how long did it take? That question is a little tougher then the first one but still a good question for someone who is looking to become a millionaire. The answer is, about 12 years."

"That's it?" Ryan said surprisingly.

"That is it," answered Steve.

"Well, I must admit that is very promising," Ryan said. I am 22 years old now, so 12 years from now I will only be 34. Who would not love being a millionaire at 34?"

Steve laughed as he hit the ball out of bounds, wide of the doubles line on the tennis court. "Not everyone can become a millionaire in 12 years; But I was fortunate enough to buy in some growing areas that really boomed, and I was able to capitalize. Once again we are moving too fast here. Let's get back to the basics and we can talk in more detail as we go through the summer.

"Now my final homework question for today was, 'what would I suggest you do to become a millionaire?' I think you know the answer to this one already but for the sake of holding up my end of the bargain, I will answer it for you. Real estate, real estate and more real estate," Steve said convincingly.

"How did I know you were going to say that!" Ryan chuckled. "However, why did you pick real estate to invest in when you were growing up?"

"Well, that is what all these lessons will be about, and when you hear this next statistic, you will know why. "When I was your age, I played basketball in the summer league in town with a guy in his early 50's named Rob Boegner. He was a big real estate investor and always drove fancy cars to the games and was always talking about his houses. He was an avid reader of real estate books and was always telling guys on the team to read some of these books. Then one day he made a comment that changed my life forever.

He said, "I'll bet you never knew that ninety percent of all millionaires in the United States earned their money in real estate."

I said "Really?" He responded with a resounding "YES!"

"Once I heard that, I figured with such high odds who would not want to do that? That was basically the day I decided I would become a real estate investor. Ever since then it has been a great ride. I have learned so much and really enjoy it."

"You're right Steve. That statistic is amazing, but aren't there all kinds of real estate investing? Isn't it risky at times?" questioned Ryan

"Yes, you are correct there are many different types of real estate investing: flipping, buying pre-construction, foreclosures, commercial, etc. However, the area that is the safest and most profitable with the least amount of risk, is easily the buy, hold and rent method. We can talk more next week. I think my hour is up and my legs are starting to wear down."

"Well, I must admit, I really got a lot of questions answered today, and I think I know what I want to do with my life," said Ryan.

"Hold on, hold on. Let's give it a few more weeks until you make a final decision," added Steve. You work on your next set of questions; I will work on this terrible backhand I have, and I'll see you on Friday, " chuckled Steve.

"You bet!" responded Ryan.

As Steve began to walk back to his car, Ryan grabbed his notebook and wrote down lesson number two.

90% of Millionaires Made Their Money in Real Estate

Chapter 4
The Leverage Of Real Estate

As the week passed, Ryan found he was wishing it was Friday again. It was almost like the other days of the week did not matter; he just looked forward to Friday nights and Monday mornings. Ryan was ready for his next lesson and was all set with his new list of questions for Steve.

As he started work Friday at *Two Brothers Pizza,* he realized Brian was not working tonight. Jimmy was working. "Jimmy what's going on? Brian usually works Friday nights," Ryan asked.

"Yes, I know, but his son is in a karate tournament tonight and asked if I could cover him," Jimmy answered.

"Okay, I just wanted to give you a heads up that there will be a delivery tonight to 600 Washington Drive that I have to take," commented Ryan.

"Steve Glass's house?" asked Jimmy.

"Yes, do you know him?" questioned Ryan.

"Yes, of course I know him. He is an electrician and has done some work for me in the past at my house," said Jimmy.

"Are you sure about that Jimmy? He told me last week he was a real estate investor." Ryan had a puzzled look on his face.

"Yes, I am positive. Why can't he be both? Look at you, you have four jobs right now."

"True, but the only full time job is here at the pizza shop. Everything else is part-time," Ryan answered.

"Well, maybe he is a part-time real estate investor or a part-time electrician," stated Jimmy.

"I guess that could be true," answered Ryan.

Then he started thinking, "how can this guy be a millionaire if he doesn't even do real estate full time. Something must be wrong here." He decided to save that question for next week because he really liked the ones he had for him this week. As the night went on, every time he came back in from a delivery he couldn't wait to see 600 Washington Drive on the delivery slip.

Sure enough it was around 8:45pm when Jimmy yelled over, "Ryan, this is the one you have been waiting for."

Once again, just like last week, Ryan snatched the pizza off the counter and away he went. Although the drive was only 5 minutes, to Ryan it seemed to take forever to get there. When he pulled up, Steve was waiting for him at the door.

"We meet again," Steve said with a smile on his face.

"We sure do," said Ryan. "I couldn't wait to get here tonight. I think I have some really good questions for us to discuss."

"Ok good. Let's hear them" asked Steve.

Ryan took a deep breath and began. "First question, why do you like real estate so much? Second question, what is the key to being successful in real estate? Third question, what kind of real estate is the best to invest in?"

"Well, I think I can handle those," answered Steve.

"Great!" Ryan exclaimed. "I'll see you Monday morning. Do me a favor Steve; try to bring a better backhand this week." He walked back to the car laughing. Steve stood at the door, shook his head, and walked back into the house.

Over the weekend, Ryan didn't think too much about his talk with Steve on real estate because his girlfriend was down for the weekend from North Jersey and a few of his college buddies drove down Saturday night to go out in Atlantic City. However, once Sunday night came around, he was excited waiting for the morning to come and was looking forward to answers to what he felt were three very important questions.

Once again when Ryan woke up Monday, it was with a little extra hop in his step and a little more energy than he was accustomed to for the early tennis shack shift. He got to the courts early and waited for Steve to show up with that atrocious backhand. Steve seemed to be running a little late today, because it was already 7:55 am and he wasn't there yet. Then Ryan saw his car pull up and he started jogging over as quickly as a guy his age could.

"Sorry Ryan, I am running a little behind today. We had some friends over this weekend, I was a little tired this morning and hit the snooze button one too many times."

"That's okay, as long as you have the answers for today I will forgive you," said Ryan.

"Can we start while you are stretching today Steve?"

"Sure, no problem at all. Okay, question #1: why do I like real estate so much? Well, this is a simple answer but a long one. There are many reasons why I like real estate, but I will try to limit my answer to a small handful because I know we don't have much time today."

"First, there is no other investment in the world where you can put up 10% of your money and get an asset worth an additional 90%. Let me explain. Most times when you buy a house, you put down 10%. However, the house you are getting is worth an additional 90%. For example, let's say you have a house for $100,000. To buy that house, it only costs you $10,000 down, but you still get an asset worth $100,000. The reason this is significant is because as the house appreciates in value, it appreciates at the 100% price that you bought it for."

"I am not quite sure I understand," answered Ryan with a puzzled look on his face.

"Here is a better example for you. For argument sake, let's say we both have $10,000 to invest. You are going to put it into the stock market, and I am going to put it into real estate," Steve said.

"Let's say you buy stock in IBM, one of the best companies in the world. It has a proven track record and over the course of time the stock has been a very strong performer. How much stock can you buy with $10,000?"

"I hope this is not a trick question" Ryan answered as he hesitated to give what he thought was a simple response. "My guess is $10,000 worth."

"That is correct!" Steve replied.

"With my $10,000, I am going to buy a $100,000 condo."

"According to many business publications, 8% is a very good return on your money, so let's use that in our example," Steve said.

"If you make an 8% return on your $10,000 of IBM stock, it will earn you $800 for the year."

"Not bad," Ryan said.

"That is true, it is not bad at all. However, if I also make an 8% return on my investment, my return is $8,000. The reason for that is because, although we both laid out $10,000 you could only purchase stock that totaled $10,000 but with my $10,000, I chose to purchase an investment worth an additional 90% more. Then in turn, my 8% return is on my total investment of $100,000 and your return is on your $10,000 investment. So after one year you received 8% return on the money you laid out but I received 80% ($8,000 against a lay out cost of $10,000) on my money," Steve said convincingly.

"Wow, that is powerful," Ryan said in a very surprising tone. "I never realized that. Now I can see why so many millionaires invest in real estate."

"Yes, but there are many other reasons why I like investing in real estate," said Steve.

"However, we will get to those, let me give you some more details on appreciation and show you how you can create wealth over time in real estate.

"We will stick with the $100,000 condo example for now in this scenario. The national average for real estate growth yearly is between 7%-9%. This varies by geography and sometimes specific markets are down or up, but you can pretty much count on a 7-9% return over the course of time on most real estate investments.

"In some cases like New York, California, and Las Vegas between 2002-2005, the return was in the 25%-40% range.

"As we have already established, an 8% return on a $100,000 condo is $8,000 for the first year. However, then the second year it will continue to increase in value another 8%. Remember this 8% is on top of the 8% from last year. For example, the first year the condo increased to $108,000 with our first year of appreciation. Then the second year it increases another 8% which would be an additional $8,640. So after two years our condo is worth $116,640.

"Over the course of time this yearly appreciation will increase more and more each year. In this scenario, in twenty years our condo will be worth $466,095.56 (using the 8% rate of return). When it comes time to sell, you are almost half way to becoming a millionaire on just this one $100,000 condo."

"I must admit, I am speechless, and that is saying a lot for a guy who spends about 8-10 hours a day talking to customers, kids and his friends," said Ryan.

"Well, let me give you a few more reasons why I like investing in real estate so much, and then we can call it a day. I know we are not getting to all three of your questions today, but I think you will agree your first question has branched us off into some good conversation," Steve added.

"Here are some more reasons why real estate is always going to be a solid investment.

"One thing in the U.S. that we can all agree on is that the population keeps going up. People are living longer lives due to medical breakthroughs, and immigration has increased. But one thing that cannot increase is land. There is only so much of it, and we cannot add some on. For these reasons, people will always need a place to live. As long as people need a place to live, real estate is and always will be a solid investment.

"Another reason it is a preferred choice in investments is because real estate is a tangible item. Unlike stocks, a property can never have its value go to $0. There have been many stocks over the past ten years that have gone bankrupt and left its investors scratching their heads. So if you put $10,000 into these stocks and they went bankrupt, you have lost all your money. In real estate you always own a tangible asset. It cannot go to $0. It might go down in value a little in a given year, but over the long haul, it is the most solid investment of all.

"Here is some more proof that real estate is a safe investment. Banks are in the business of lending money. They cannot make money unless they lend money. If real estate was not a safe investment why would banks be willing to give you an asset (house) if you are only risking 10% of your money and in turn they are risking 90% of their money?"

"That makes a lot of sense," responded Ryan.

"One last thing in comparison to stocks. When you buy a stock, you are betting on a company or trusting your broker that they have done the research and proper evaluation for you. You really have no idea what goes on inside that particular company or what will go on in the future.

"However, when you buy real estate, you are betting on yourself and your own research, analysis, and instincts." Steve concluded. "You pick where to buy, what to buy, and what price to pay. These are all decisions you make prior to the purchase. You are setting the rules and boundaries for your own investment."

"Well, that sure was a mouthful, and you are right, I don't think I want answers to questions #2 and #3 right now. I have a lot to take in after your response to my first question today," Ryan responded in a tone that appeared a little exhausted.

"We can pick this back up on Friday night with your list," Steve said. "Don't worry, today's lesson is probably the longest one we have. It was important for me to get you to understand why investing in real estate is so beneficial and why it creates so many more opportunities than other types of investments."

"Well, it has definitely peaked my attention, that is for sure. I'm beginning to feel like you are getting the short end of the stick in our deal. So, here is a lesson for you. When you go to play a shot off your backhand side, you must change your grip about a half an inch so that your stroke from the backhand can accommodate the different swing from your forehand," Ryan offered.

"Oh really," said Steve. "I never realized that. Maybe that explains why most of my backhand shots go in the net," he laughed.

"You got it," said Ryan. "I'll see you on Friday and thanks for the great information. I appreciate it.

"No problem Ryan. Maybe next week you can show me how I can improve my net play."

"Count on it," Ryan said with a smile.

As Steve walked toward his car, Ryan once again got out his notebook and wrote down his next lesson.

In Real Estate, 10% Investment Buys You 100% of Product

Chapter 5
What Makes You A Millionaire In Real Estate?

Although it was another busy week for Ryan with two basketball games and work, he was still anxious to ask Steve his next two questions. Obviously, two of his questions from last week would be included tonight plus an additional one was added to his list.

The town had now hit full summer stride and the island was as crazy as it could be. The population doubled in the summer and from Ryan's standpoint, the vacation drivers could use a few driving lessons. However, over the years he had learned to be a little more patient on the road in the summer and he constantly kept telling himself, the higher the population, the more deliveries, the more deliveries, the more tips. Sometimes it was hard for Ryan to stick to that mind set, especially after he was cut off a few times, but he got used to it and never really let it bother him.

In the summer, on Friday nights, *Two Brothers Pizza* had five delivery drivers instead of the usual three for non-summer months. The good news for Ryan was that the pizza shop was busy, the bad news was, it was harder to ensure that he would get the 600 Washington Drive delivery. Although Brian and Jimmy knew the situation, it was not always up to them. The girls that covered the phones behind the counter sometimes would setup the deliveries because Brian and Jimmy were swamped making pies in both ovens.

As the delivery drivers sat there waiting to begin their shift, Ryan thought it would be a good idea to make sure everyone knew he needed the delivery to Steve's house. "Hey guys, tonight there will be a delivery to 600 Washington Drive that I need to take," Ryan said to the group who was getting their money ready to make change for customers for the upcoming shift.

"Why you?" said Rich. "Is he a good tipper?"

"Well, he is a good tipper, but that is not the reason. I am helping him with some tennis lessons and he is helping me with a summer project," Ryan answered.

"I'll do it if you split the tip," scoffed Rich.

"Are you serious?" Ryan responded. "Fine, I will give you half of whatever the tip is, if the address shows up in your delivery pile tonight."

Although Ryan was a little annoyed, it was to his advantage. First, most people on the island tipped between $1-$2 and since Steve more than doubled that, he was still going to end up getting a decent tip. Plus, Ryan would have probably agreed to give Rich the whole tip if he asked because he just wanted to continue the lessons with Steve and hopefully learn enough to begin his quest on becoming a millionaire.

It was a crazy night again in the pizza shop. All five delivery guys coming and going and by 10:00 Ryan had already made 47 deliveries. Then about 10:10 Rich yelled over, "Ryan, this is the one you have been waiting for. Don't forget, I get half the tip."

"Trust me, I didn't forget. Thanks for giving it to me," Ryan said.

This Friday night, Steve's order was not the usual. Instead of Steve's regular large pizza, he had a small pizza and a few sandwiches.

When Ryan pulled up to Steve's house this time, there were a few cars in the driveway. He walked up the walkway and knocked on the door. Steve answered with a Phillies hat on backwards.

"Hey Ryan, what's up?" Steve said.

"Not much, are you having a party here tonight?" Ryan asked.

"No, not a party but a few of my friends came over to watch the Phillies Mets game."

"That is a shame that you and your friends waste time watching inferior baseball. You should know by now there is only one team worth watching, the Yanks," Ryan said with confidence.

"Be careful Ryan, you are one comment away from losing the rest of your education this summer," Steve responded.

"Ok, ok" answered Ryan. "Remember I have two questions left over from last week plus one additional. Here they are:

"First, what is the key to being successful in real estate? Second, what kind of real estate is the best to invest in? Third, how do I know what properties are good ones?"

"Once again, I think I can handle these three questions on Monday. I will be ready Ryan, and I plan on using your tip from last week on my grip for my backhand," answered Steve.

"Okay, see you then," Ryan said as he walked away with a smile on his face back to the car.

Monday morning started out cloudy and a little chilly. Beach was known for being windy, even in the summer, and when it was cloudy it got a little cold for a summer day. On cloudy days it was tougher for Ryan to get up and get to the tennis shack early. He knew there would be hardly anyone playing but he still had to be there in case there were a few crazy patrons trying to get in their exercise for the day. To be honest, he was more concerned about Steve coming down.

Then suddenly, at about 7:45, Ryan saw Steve's car pull up. Steve got out of the car slowly and headed over to the shack.

"Well, it was tough getting up today Ryan, I must admit." Steve said.

"Is that because of the weather or because the Phillies got swept by the Mets?" Ryan asked with a chuckle.

"Very funny," Steve added. "Actually, it was probably both, but I knew we had scheduled this meeting. However, today would have been a good day to stay in bed."

"Ok, let's get started Ryan because I might not be able to stay the whole hour today; I have some paperwork I need to finish at home for one of my properties."

"Speaking of that, can I ask you a quick question before we start? Are you an electrician?" Ryan asked.

"Yes, I am. I am a real estate investor part-time and an electrician part-time," answered Steve.

"Why would you still be an electrician part time if you are a millionaire?" asked Ryan.

"Well, I like it. Plus I make my own hours and only take jobs that I want to do. Most of the work I do now is for my friends or acquaintances," responded Steve.

"That doesn't make sense to me," added Ryan. "If you are a millionaire, why work at all?"

"Being a millionaire should not change who you are. It might change how you live a little, but if you like to work, you would not be happy just doing nothing all day. Every millionaire has his or her own agenda. Some play golf 5 days a week, others still work part-time jobs to keep busy, and others spend 20-30 hours a week doing community service. It all depends on what you like to do.

"However, being a millionaire gives you many more options. You can choose how much and how long to work. You can choose how you want to spend your time. Let me give you an example.

"You mentioned you teach the kids' recreation programs in town, correct?" asked Steve. "Why do you do it?"

"I do it because I enjoy teaching the kids about sports and seeing their excitement," answered Ryan.

"Exactly!" exclaimed Steve. "So if you hit the lottery tonight and you won $5 million dollars would you get up and teach them tomorrow?"

"I am sure I would," smiled Ryan.

"Of course you would because you like doing that and you would continue to do it," claimed Steve.

"Any other questions before I give you the answers to my homework?" asked Steve.

"Nope, we are all set," answered Ryan.

"Okay, first question, 'what is the key to being successful in real estate?' This is an easy one. The key to being successful in real estate is TENANTS!" exclaimed Steve.

"Tenants are what make you a millionaire in real estate. Here is the best way to explain it. How would you like it if you had someone pay all your bills and expenses for a house that continued to appreciate in value?" questioned Steve.

"I think that would be great," Ryan answered.

"Of course you would, who wouldn't? That is what renting is all about. Tenants pay rent to you, which covers the mortgage, taxes, water, sewer, insurance, lawn care and any other miscellaneous charges required to run the house. The best part is, not only are they paying all your expenses to run the house while it appreciates in value but the mortgage is also being paid down at the same time. Think about the condo example from last week. If you had a 30-year mortgage and wanted to sell the condo in 20 years, you are not only benefiting from the projected appreciation of 7%-9%, but the mortgage you have to pay off when you sell the property will be significantly less then when you purchased the home which adds to your profit," said Steve.

"That makes perfect sense," responded Ryan.

"It sure does," confirmed Steve. "Remember, your tenants will make you a millionaire. Consider your tenants, not as friends, but as business partners. What I mean by that is treat them with respect and loyalty but also ensure that you have strict rules and regulations with regard to the property and its use. We are getting a little ahead of ourselves again; I will save that for another week. I am freezing out here, let's move on to your second question.

"Okay, question #2. 'What kind of real estate is the best to invest in?' I am going to give you a totally biased opinion on this one Ryan. In my opinion, residential real estate is the best real estate to invest in. There is money to be made in all kinds of real estate, but residential is the most common and the most in demand. As we discussed before, people always need a place to live and residential real estate provides that. Now, as far as condos, duplexes or single family homes, that is a subject for a later discussion, but they all fall under the residential real estate umbrella."

"That sounds pretty basic," Ryan answered.

"It is basic. Don't worry we will get into more details on what to look for and where, next week. However, that pretty much summarizes the second question. Now that I answered two questions, I think we need to table the third question until next week since that deals with the next phase of your education."

"That is fine with me" responded Ryan. "I will put that on the top of my list with a few more for Friday."

"Hopefully, it will be a little warmer next week or I might only answer one question before I get going," answered Steve.

Ryan laughed and then slowly walked back to the tennis shack. Once he got inside he grabbed his notebook and wrote down his newest lesson.

Tenants are What Make You a Millionaire in Real Estate

Chapter 6
Positive Cash Flow

By the time Monday afternoon rolled around, Ryan was very excited. He kept glancing at his notebook and started to piece together his talks with Steve. He really liked what he had learned so far. The one thing he kept going back to after each of their meetings was the fact that some of these tips (or secrets depending on how you look at it) were not rocket science. He knew he was a long way from becoming a millionaire, but after a few pizza deliveries to Steve and a few tennis lessons, he felt he was well on his way.

That night after work, he went to Pop's house to give him an update on how things were going with his summer project.

"Hey Pop!"

"Hey pal, how it is going?" Pop responded.

"As good as can be" Ryan answered. "Looks like you are watching the Yanks. What's the score? They were down three to two after six innings when I left work."

"How are they doing? They are driving me nuts, that's how they are doing. When I played the game, if the score was close it was automatic that the runner would be bunted over. Now, with all the glamour of home runs and smaller ballparks, everyone swings for the fences. The Yanks could have moved four runners over so far tonight, but every attempt ended in an out."

"Pop, when are you going to get into the twenty-first century. With the money these guys are making, you think a 40 home run hitter is going to lay down a bunt?" Ryan said.

"The great game of baseball is not just about home runs. It is about playing it the right way, doing what the team needs to win. That is what I have been trying to teach you and your brother for years," yelled Pop.

"Come on Pop, you know I am a good bunter," Ryan joked.

"Hey, I stopped by to give you an update on my summer project that we talked about a few weeks ago," added Ryan.

"How is it going? Did you find any millionaires?" Pop questioned.

"It is going great! I did find one millionaire so far, and he might be all I need. I found a real estate investor, and he is as sharp as a tack," Ryan said.

"Real estate investor? Then he is smart. Real estate is always been a great investment. Actually, I wish growing up, I would have been a little smarter and invested in real estate. Your Nanny tried to talk me into that about 30 years ago, and I pushed it off at the time. I sure do regret it now." Pop continued. "We bought a few houses in our life, and they turned out great. Every time we sold, we made a big profit which helped us purchase the next house."

"Well, I still have a lot to learn but I think I will be ready once the summer ends," responded Ryan.

"When is your next game?" Pop asked

"Tomorrow at 7:30 pm. We play the Bulldogs," answered Ryan.

"Ok, I'll be there."

"Sounds good Pop. I have to run, I am supposed to meet my brother out for some wings. I'll see you tomorrow," Ryan said as he put his baseball cap on backwards and walked out the door.

The one thing Ryan had to work on before Friday was a few more questions. He knew he had one from last week they would review but he needed two more. He thought it was time to ask some questions that could help him get to the heart of investing. Where do you get the money to invest? What do I look for? What determines a good price? He made a list of questions and then figured he would have a few days to narrow it down.

By the time Friday came, Ryan was exhausted. Since he was headed into the middle of the summer, the bar and grill was busy almost every night due to the summer crowd in town. In turn, the owner asked him to work a few extra nights this week. He never minded because most of the time his friends were there anyway.

As his Friday night pizza shift started, he got a little energy back thinking about Steve and his next three questions. Ryan was really expecting one of his next few lessons to break the bank and get him going on his quest to be a millionaire.

Sure enough, right on schedule, Jimmy called out at around 10:20 pm, "Ryan, 600 Washington Drive."

Ryan jumped up off the stool and pounced on that pie like a pitcher trying to field a bunt on a squeeze play. As he stepped into the car he grabbed his notebook and circled the questions for tonight.

"Knock, Knock," Ryan said.

"Come on in Ryan, I am trying to find my wallet," replied Steve.

"I have my list ready," Ryan yelled, as Steve was somewhere upstairs looking for some money to pay for the pizza.

"Shoot," Steve said as he came walking down the steps with his wallet in his hand, digging through it looking for a twenty.

"Okay, first is really our third question from last week. How do I know what properties are good ones? Second, where do I look for these properties? Third what do I do once I find a property I like?" Ryan asked.

"Now we're talking," said Steve. "Sounds like we are getting close to cutting you loose. These are good questions to ask before looking for a place. I will be ready Monday with these answers. Thanks for the pizza and have a great weekend," responded Steve.

"Okay, later," Ryan said as he headed back to his car and the pizza shop.

When Monday rolled around there was good news and bad news. The good news was it was hot and sunny. The bad news was it rained all night on Sunday and Ryan was stuck pushing the squeegee across all the courts trying to get the water off so people could play. When Steve arrived, he had only finished five of the eight courts.

"Sorry Steve, I didn't realize the courts would be this wet today. I can't play until I get all the courts clear," Ryan said with a disappointed tone in his voice.

"No problem," answered Steve. "I'll grab one of those squeegee's from the shack and help you and we can talk while we clear the courts.'

"Wow, thanks a lot Steve!"

"No problem. Let's get started with our questions from Friday. Okay, first: 'how do you know what properties are good ones?' The answer to this question could be the single most important lesson I teach you. As much as it is a simple answer and makes perfect sense, many people don't follow it."

"Any property that can produce positive cash flow is a 'good' property. What I mean by that is, after you research all the properties' expenses, the mortgage, taxes, insurance, water and sewer, etc. and the rents cover all these charges, it is then considered a 'good property.' It is even acceptable to have a property break even on a monthly basis.

"Remember, our value in the property is going to come from appreciation over time and our tenants paying down our mortgage, so as long as we don't have to lay out money each month, it is a good property. I even have two properties now that are a little negative each month, minus $42 and the other one is minus $56. Now I know these two properties are in a good area that is growing so I don't mind laying out a total expense of $98 a month because I know it is appreciating at a far greater rate than that each month."

"I am starting to see how all these tie into each other," Ryan answered with a smile on his face.

"You got it!" said Steve. "Let me elaborate a little on this point to make sure you get the right idea. There are thousands of properties on this island that do not fall into this category. Depending on where you are in the US, some markets can be very difficult to find a property that can cover all its expenses. You really need to search, research, and try to find a good deal. In some cases you might need to buy a duplex or triplex to get to a break-even point. This gives you the ability to get additional rents to help cover these expenses on a monthly basis."

"I understand." Ryan said as he pushed the squeegee under the fence with two inches of water in front of it.

"We will go in more detail later on that question but let's move on to question #2. 'Where do you look for these properties?' This is where your pizza delivery skills will excel," Steve said with a grin on his face that spread from ear to ear.

"You are losing me again Steve," Ryan said with a puzzled look.

"You drive around all day on this island delivering pizzas. I am sure you know every street in town and probably many of the house addresses by heart," questioned Steve.

"That is true. I can even tell you house colors in about 90% of the deliveries," Ryan answered.

"Exactly!" Steve said. "I am sure you know more about real estate on this island then you even think you know. If I asked you where you thought a good place to buy that might be affordable and is an up and coming part of town, I am pretty sure you could give me an answer in 5 minutes. Is that true?" asked Steve.

"I have a few places I think are on the rise in this town," answered Ryan.

"That is exactly my point. You ride around all day and see the different types of houses, condos, duplexes, and apartments in town. You know who lives in each one, what the neighborhoods are like, and what areas are growing. You are so far ahead of the game, and you don't even know it."

"I never really thought about that," Ryan said.

"Your homework for this week is to look at the island a little differently. I want you to look for areas or spots that you think would be good places to buy. Remember, to be a good investor, it helps to be an expert in the area you want to invest in. I think it is safe to say you are an expert on knowing this island."

"Sounds like a plan. I will get right on it." Ryan answered.

"Remember, there is an old real estate adage that has been around for hundreds of years. 'The three most important items in real estate are location, location, location.'

"Let's move on to your third question for this week. 'What do I do once I find a property I like?' I think I am going to change this question around a little. Instead of asking 'What do I do once I find a property I like,' let's change that to: 'What do I do once I find a property I am interested in.' The difference between the two is that we don't like a property until we know the expenses and know it will have positive cash flow or at least break even. In order to do that, we need to get information on the house, like the taxes, insurance, the monthly fees etc. Then we run the numbers and find out if it is a potential purchase. If we run the numbers and the house would be running at a negative cash flow of $150 a month, then we cross this property off our list and move onto to another one."

"So basically you are saying, even if you think an area is growing or in a good part of town, if you cannot break even then it is not a 'good' property? Ryan asked.

"That is exactly what I am saying. It might be a nice house to live in, but from a pure investment standpoint, it is not a good property for real estate investors," answered Steve.

"Remember, we want tenants to make us millionaires by paying all our expenses. If we buy properties in which we are paying some of the expenses then that is defeating the purpose," Steve added.

"I never thought of it that way," Ryan answered

"Well, I think that wraps up this lesson. At least somebody else will get to play on these tennis courts today, now that we have cleaned them off," laughed Steve.

"Thanks again for all your help with the real estate and the courts," added Ryan.

"See you on Friday," Steve said

"You can count on it," Ryan yelled from the tennis shack.

Ryan then grabbed his notebook and wrote down the two lessons of the today.

Find Properties with Positive Cash Flow and you are on Your Way to Becoming a Millionaire

To Be a Good Investor; It Helps to Be an Expert in the Area You Are Investing

Chapter #7
Finding A
Down Payment

This week was much different then any of the other weeks during Ryan's summer project. Although he still had to get some questions together for Steve, he spent most of his day delivering pizzas and looking at neighborhoods and houses around town trying to decide what he thought would be a good investment. He was still in the dark about real estate, but he figured nobody drives around the island more than he does so he would attempt to find a place that would gain Steve's approval.

At first it seemed weird. He drove this island hundreds if not thousands of times, but this week it looked different. He tried to really focus on areas or neighborhoods that he thought would increase in value over time or ones that looked like they were on the rise.

By the time Friday morning came, he really started to think how much of an advantage he had by being a pizza delivery driver. Because he passed almost every house every day, he would know what houses went up for sale almost immediately. He knew the neighborhoods on the island, and he also knew most of the neighbors in those neighborhoods. By the time Friday came he felt very comfortable with what he was looking for. That didn't mean Ryan found anything yet, but he knew what he was looking for and sometimes that can be half the battle.

Ryan was so busy looking at houses on the island that he only prepared two questions for Steve for Friday night. Once again, he tried to prepare questions that he thought were a little more complex as they continued to talk in more detail about real estate.

While he was waiting for a delivery, Jimmy yelled over from the oven, "Ryan, I have two extra tickets to the Phillies game tomorrow, do you want to go?"

"I don't think so Jimmy. As much as I love baseball, I have a tough time watching games between the Phillies and the Padres," replied Ryan.

"Okay, suit yourself," Jimmy answered.

"Thanks for the offer, Jimmy," Ryan said.

"Well, looks like your timing is perfect; here is our weekly 600 Washington Drive delivery," Jimmy said as he put the slip with the address in the pizza holder.

As Ryan headed toward Washington Drive, he continued to keep his eyes peeled for any house that he thought would be a good investment. Although he had an area in mind, he was hoping to find another one to talk to Steve about.

"Guess who," Ryan called as he knocked on the screen door.

"I am pretty sure I can guess," Steve answered with a chuckle in his voice.

"What did you get here, a stromboli?" asked Ryan.

"Yes I did, my buddy Mel told me *Two Brothers Pizza* makes a great stromboli and I should try it one day. So I thought, why not today?"

"Did you bring me my homework ?" asked Steve.

"You know I did," answered Ryan. "However, I only have two questions this week because I spent most of my time this week looking for *good investments* around town."

"That is fine with me," Steve answered.

"First, how can I get the money to purchase these properties? Second, what kind of property should I try to buy first?"

"These are very good questions. I am starting to think I am a good teacher," joked Steve. "I'll be ready on Monday. Hopefully, we get a chance to play some tennis this week."

"That makes two of us," responded Ryan. "Talk to you Monday, Steve".

"I'll be there with my killer serve," laughed Steve.

Monday turned out to be another windy day in town. Although it was not raining or even cloudy for that matter, it was still not considered ideal tennis weather. Steve pulled into the parking lot at 7:50 am. He waltzed over to the tennis shack with a big grin on his face.

"What are you so happy about," Ryan said.

"What are you talking about? The Phillies have won four in a row and have a make up double header today. Who wouldn't be happy about that?" asked Steve. "Okay, let's jump right in."

Ryan was ready. "First, how can I get the money to purchase these properties?"

"There are many answers to this question;" Steve replied. Some answers are creative and some are standard. However, I will tell you some of the things that I do and then you can decide what method best fits you and your needs.

"The first and easiest one if you have it, is to use your savings. Many people don't have $10,000 or $20,000 in the bank but there are some people who do."

"Well, hopefully you have some better ideas than that," Ryan said.

"I said this was the easiest one, not the most common or the one I use most frequently," answered Steve.

"Let me ask you a question. How much do you save from your jobs each week?" asked Steve.

"Not much, if any at all, answered Ryan.

"Why do you think that is?" asked Steve.

"For one thing, I am still young and spend most of my money going out with my friends or my girlfriend or on things I like. Like Yankee games, golf, or vacations." answered Ryan.

"What if you never saw a portion of that money in your paycheck. Do you think you would miss it ?" asked Steve.

"I am sure I would. Who wouldn't," claimed Ryan.

"Well, you would be surprised. Actually the opposite it true. If your paycheck is between 10%-20% less than it is today and you never saw the money, you would never miss it. Many people think they need every penny of their paycheck to live week to week but in actuality, when people setup a forced saving from their paycheck for between 10%-20% a week, it only takes them one paycheck before they change their spending habits and the savings begin.

"Let me explain how this works. Anytime you have money in your pocket, or in your checking account, you always are thinking of things to do, and what to spend, knowing that the next paycheck is only seven days away. However, if a small portion of that is missing from your account, you are never looking for it. I have used this savings method for years and I know thousands of people who do the same. It is the easiest way to have your savings accumulate quickly to help with a down payment. Many companies around the world adopted this method for their employees through the companies 401K plans.

"Many employers ask the employees how much (percentage) they would like to contribute into their 401K plan. Then the employer takes that percentage right out of the employees paycheck and puts it right in the employees 401K account.

"The employee never sees the money and it is being put away for a good reason, retirement. Same thing can happen with people who don't work for big companies. You need to find a way to setup a forced saving situation in which you never see the money in your paycheck. Then after 6-8 months when you look in there, you will be amazed at what you see. It is a simple plan, 'Can't spend what you don't see,' said Steve.

"I am not sure I can do that but I am willing to try," stated Ryan.

"How much of your paycheck from *Two Brothers Pizza* is your overall weekly pay? Please include in this figure, the tennis shack, the bar and grill and the recreation programs," said Steve.

"Hold on let me calculate," answered Ryan. "Well if you only include my salary and not my tips, about 19%."

"Perfect. This is what I want you to do. Open a saving account this week at the same bank that *Two Brothers Pizza* does their banking. Then fill out deposits slips for your account and give it to Brian. Then ask him when he goes to make the deposits for the business if he can deposit your check, which is about 19% of your overall salary, into your saving account. Knowing Brian, he will not have a problem with it. Then in no time you will have saved enough money for your down payment."

"You really think that is going to work?" Ryan asked.

"You have met me here for over a month, are you beginning to doubt me now?" joked Steve.

"No, I am just not familiar with the idea I guess," answered Ryan.

"Okay, here are some other ways to get down payments to purchase real estate. The next method I use and have used a number of times is taking a home equity loan out against my current home.

"I can do this since the interest is tax deductible and most people who have lived in their home for more than five years have some significant equity in the house. Since you don't own a house yet, we don't have to spend much time on this method, but in the future it is surely one you can benefit from.

"The next method I have used on more than one occasion is to borrow the money from family or friends. However, this can be very tricky. I know many friends who have horror stories about borrowing from family, but if you do it professionally, efficiently and business-like it can be a win / win situation. Let me explain.

Let's say your grandfather is retired and living off a fixed income. This probably means he has some of his money tied up in CDs which generally pay a very low return on your money. It is safe and guaranteed but the return is still very low. Because the return is so low you have an opportunity to create a win / win situation for both of you. Let me use an example from one of my deals. My grandfather had $6,000 in a CD that was earning him 2% interest a year. When I found that out, I asked him if he would be interested in earning double that amount on his money. Of course he said, "yes," and I offered him double that amount yearly. So in this case he went from making 2% a year on his money to now making 4% a year. He doubled his money, and I was able to borrow money for a down payment.

"Now we already know we can buy 100% product with only 10% down so I would make the money I borrowed back from him in less than one year. In turn, he is happy and I am happy. He gets double his interest and I get the house.

"The part that usually causes the problem is how the agreement is documented. If you just take the money from him and tell him you will pay him back when you can, you are looking for a problem. He might be expecting it at one time and you are planning to pay it back another time.

"This is the best thing to do when borrowing from friends or family.

"Create a one page contract in letter format. The letter should clearly state how much the loan is for, the terms of the loan and the payoff date. Also include in the letter the exact amount of the payoff with interest. I also suggest two other items. First, I suggest you use three to five years if possible for the loan to give you plenty of time to earn back the money plus more. Second, make sure you include a clause that clearly details if something happens to the lender (i.e. passes away, etc.). This will help in any family disputes or questions about the loan. I usually have a clause that states 'If anything happens to "the lender" between now and the payoff time, the money with interest will be paid back to his wife on the agreed upon settlement date.'

"The final step of this agreement is to make sure you have two copies and both of you sign each copy. One for him and one for you. It is important to have two copies to ensure that both parties are looking and seeing the same contract."

"I like this idea!" exclaimed Ryan.

"I am not sure if I have any friends or relatives that have their money in CDs, but if I can offer them double their money why wouldn't they take it?"

"To be honest, most times they will take it, especially people who are on fixed incomes," responded Steve.

"There are also other ways to get down payments that would be covered in the real estate investing 202 next year, which would include things like, financing 100% of the property with the bank, or asking the seller to hold the down payment portion as a loan between you and him. However, I think you get the idea. Getting a down payment is not as impossible as most people make it out to be."

"Not when you explain it that way," Ryan said.

"Let's move on to your second question, 'What kind of property should you try to buy first?' This is a tough question because it depends on what kind of deal you find. Just off the top of my head, I would like you to try to buy a condo. Since you are still a novice in the investing business, a condo could be the perfect fit. There are many benefits of a condo. First, you pay a monthly condominium association fee which usually covers insurance, maintenance, lawn care, snow removal, and even sometimes heat. These are many items that you would have to handle yourself or pay someone to handle. A condo is something that usually does not require much maintenance because that is handled by the association, so you don't have to worry about the roof or the heating unit or the bushes in front of your unit.

"However, some people do not like condos. Some condominiums have strict rules on renting and have fees that some owners don't want to pay. So each type of real estate investment has pros and cons but to start, I think I would still suggest a condo," Steve said convincingly.

"Well, I will not get my heart set on a condo, but I will lean towards it. How is that?" Ryan asked.

"That sounds like a good plan," answered Steve. "Okay, before I go, how did your search go in finding an area or neighborhood where you think you would like to make a purchase?"

"I think I found some areas I am confident will continue to appreciate. However, I think I am going to take the lessons from today and try to combine them with what I was looking for last week before I ask what you think," smiled Ryan.

"That is fine. However, there is one more thing I want you to work on this week. When you find a place you like, I want you to look in the paper and see if any houses or condos are for sale in that area. If they are, call the realtor and ask some questions like, how much are the taxes, how much is the sewer and water, and how old is the house. Then we can run some numbers to determine if it is something you should look at," Steve said.

"Sounds good to me. I will do that this week." Ryan responded.

"I think that about does it for today. Another successful lesson and I swear my backhand is getting better," chuckled Steve.

"It is, don't worry," laughed Ryan.

As the sweat dripped down his face, Ryan wiped his brow on his shirt, grabbed his pen and notebook and wrote down the day's lesson.

You Can't Spend What You Don't See, Forced Savings

Chapter 8
Time = Money

That same day on his way home from the tennis shack, Ryan stopped into the convenience store and picked up a copy of the local paper. He figured between deliveries he could glance through the paper and see what houses were for sale on the island. He could also make a call or two if he found one that he thought was a potential investment.

Since his meeting with Steve on Monday, Ryan felt he had a lot to accomplish in four days before his next delivery to Steve on Friday night. On Tuesday morning, after the recreation programs, Ryan went to Beach Savings Bank to open an account per Steve's recommendation. He opened the account with $100 and left there with a good feeling that he was really making progress in his real estate education. After he opened the account he headed off to the pizza shop.

"Hey Jimmy, what's going on?" Ryan asked as he walked in the door about 20 minutes before his shift started.

"Not much. You're early today," Jimmy answered with a surprised look on his face. "I haven't seen you in this early since you forgot to put your clock back in the last daylight saving time," laughed Jimmy.

"Very funny, very funny," Ryan said with a smile on his face. "I wanted to talk to you for a minute and ask you and Brian for a favor."

"No problem, what is it?" Jimmy asked.

"Well, I just opened a saving account at Beach Savings Bank across the street and was wondering if it was possible that when you make the deposits for the business if you could also deposit my full paycheck in my account? I already have the deposit slips filled out. You just have to put the amount and the date."

"Forced savings, I like it" answered Jimmy.

"Yes, how did you know that?" asked Ryan.

"Someone explained that to me and Brian a long time ago when we first bought this business. Wait until you see how fast your savings account grows when you don't see the money," responded Jimmy. "No problem, we can do that for you."

"Thanks Jimmy, I owe you one." Ryan said.

"I'll put that on your tab," Jimmy said as he rolled his eyes and walked in the back to get the rest of the pizza supplies for the day.

It was still about 15 minutes before Ryan's shift began. He decided to sit in one of the booths and start looking in the paper to see if he could find anything that he thought could be a good investment. As he was sitting there, the door opened and Steve walked in.

"I was hoping I would catch you here," said Steve as he walked over to the booth.

"Hey Steve, what's going on?" Ryan asked.

"I keep forgetting to mention to you that I am taking my kids and wife on vacation to Disney World for two weeks starting Saturday," answered Steve.

"But don't worry, I am not leaving you high and dry. I am going to have a substitute fill in for me for two weeks," continued Steve.

"Substitute?" Ryan asked.

"Yes, I have asked one of my friends who I am also partners with if he could substitute for me for two weeks until I get back. I think you know him. It's Mel Bodine," added Steve.

"You mean Mel Bodine, the teacher?" Ryan asked with a very surprised look on his face. "The man who lives at 100 Oggi Avenue in the green house with tan shutters?"

"Yes, that's him. He teaches seventh grade math. Didn't you have him as a teacher?" Steve inquired.

"Yes I did," answered Ryan.

"By the way how did you know what color house he lived in?" asked Steve with a puzzled look on his face.

"He is a *Two Brother Pizza* regular. He orders two large pizzas every Wednesday night, one pizza with pepperoni and other one plain. Plus I have taught his kids in the recreation programs a few times," Ryan answered.

"But hold on, I don't think I understand. If I needed help with math I could see sitting with Mr. Bodine for a few hours but we are talking about real estate," Ryan said.

"Ha, you are still so naïve and innocent," responded Steve. "Mel is a real estate investor. I think he now owns about six or seven properties. I am not sure if he is *officially* a millionaire yet, but I am sure he will be soon."

"That is very interesting," Ryan said.

"That being said, I want to just review a few small items before I go on my trip with you. Instead of our Friday question session how about you bring a large pizza over on Thursday night when you get off, and I can cover them before I get ready to leave. In the meantime, I will tell Mel you are going to be stopping by to setup some time with him for the next two weeks."

"That sounds good to me," answered Ryan. "I get off at 10:00 pm on Thursday, is that too late?"

"No, I am sure I will be watching the last few innings of the Phillies game," Steve said.

"You mean you are going to put me through that torture on Thursday?" Ryan joked.

"Very funny, Ryan," answered Steve. "Okay, then we are on for Thursday night around ten."

"You got it," Ryan answered.

It was Wednesday around 5:15 pm when Ryan grabbed a handful of deliveries and loaded them in the car. Once he got them in the car he looked to see what is the best route to take and in which order. When he looked down at the two pies he saw Mel's address, 100 Oggi Avenue. "Nice," he said to himself. He immediately decided that would be the first delivery out of the next set.

When he pulled up to the house, Mel's two kids were on the lawn throwing the baseball around.

"Hey guys. How are those swings coming?" Ryan asked.

"So far so good," the older one answered. "Dad, the pizza is here," he yelled into the house.

Mel came to the door with his wallet in hand.

"Hey Ryan, come on in," Mel said.

"Thanks Mel," Ryan responded.

"I hear I have some summer school classes to teach over the next two weeks," laughed Mel.

"Yes, I spoke with Steve yesterday, he said you could substitute for him for two weeks while he is gone," replied Ryan.

"That is no problem. When is a good time?" asked Mel.

"Whatever is good for you," said Ryan.

"Do you have some free time on Fridays around lunch time" questioned Mel?

"Well, I work at the pizza shop starting at 12:00 but I am free before that." replied Ryan.

"Let's shoot for 11:00 am at the pizza shop. We can talk over lunch and cover a few items that Steve asked me to cover with you. We can do that for two weeks until he comes back," Mel said.

"Ok, I will put it in my date book. Friday 11:00 am, pizza shop."

"Ok great, I will see you then Ryan."

"Thanks Mel," Ryan said as he walked back to the car.

When Ryan got back in the car, he added this appointment in his date book and crossed off the next two Monday mornings.

The next day and a half Ryan tried to read the paper and look around the island for a good investment. He thought he finally found a spot on the island that he thought was an area that was on the rise and decided this will be the area he will try to find something to buy. He also found a few condos for sale in that area and thought it was affordable and potentially a home run. However, he would need to call the agents to get additional information on the condos so he could run the numbers to see if they would work.

It was now Thursday around 9:30 pm.

"Brian, do me a favor. I need a large pie with sausage to go when my shift ends," Ryan said.

"No problem Ryan," Brian responded.

It was now 9:55, and Ryan had cashed in all his slips and was officially off the clock. He grabbed the sausage pizza, hopped in the car, and was off to Steve's house. When he got there all the lights were off except the living room. He walked up to the door and knocked lightly. Steve opened the door with his fingers pointing over his lip gesturing to be quiet.

"Hey Steve," Ryan whispered.

"Hey, Ryan, the kids just went down. I have been trying to get them to sleep for over an hour."

They should be asleep in 5 more minutes and then we can talk like regular human beings. Can you please bring the pizza into the kitchen?" asked Steve.

"No problem," Ryan replied.

Then Steve walked upstairs for a few minutes and then came back down with a look that was a cross between happy and relieved.

"Okay, are we all set?" asked Steve.

"You tell me," responded Ryan.

"Today I didn't want you to bring any questions because there are a few loose ends I wanted to cover with you before I left. Plus, I wanted to talk to you about what topics Mel will be covering for me while I am away. Most of the items we have covered so far will be able to get you through the basics of real estate investing and definitely get you well on your way to becoming a millionaire. However, I wanted to put your mind at ease on a few things we didn't get into thoroughly.

"I know over the past few weeks you have been trying to find that perfect place to invest in. Although, there is much research that is needed before a purchase is made, you don't always have to find a *perfect* deal. All deals that have positive cash flow or break even on expenses are all good deals over time. Real estate is slow moving. Not like stocks. There is no need to watch the market every second of the day. Time will take care of the property. In real estate Time = Money. The longer you hold a property, the more money you will make on it. Remember, the longer you hold it, the more mortgage payments your tenants pay, which lowers your payoff amount and in turn makes a bigger the profit for you."

"This philosophy does not hold true in flipping transaction, but we are not focused on that kind of investing. That is too risky and you can really get caught on the wrong side of a deal in a tough market."

"Time = Money," Ryan replied. "That is a good point and one that is simple to remember."

"Yes, one of the other things I wanted to bring up on why real estate is such a great investment is because it plays no favorites. It can be for the younger generation, the older generation and everyone in between. You can start early in your life or later in your life and still benefit greatly from real estate. I know people who didn't invest in real estate until they were retired and are now building fortunes with the houses they have purchased."

"I can see that," Ryan answered. "If someone was able to retire a little early, say around 55 or so, they can still buy a house and live to see it be paid off in 20-30 years."

"Exactly," said Steve.

"The last things I wanted to cover with you before I leave are the topics I have asked Mel to review with you while I am gone. He is going to cover two very important lessons, which I believe he is an expert on.

Those two topics are Partners and Tenants. He has a lot of experience in both areas and is sure to help you understand what to look for in each and how to protect yourself from each."

"I already have two appointments set up with him on the next two Fridays at 11:00 am at the pizza shop," answered Ryan.

"Ok, good. Don't worry. He is a great guy with plenty of knowledge to share. You will enjoy him over the next two weeks and then when I get back we can pick up where we left off. To be honest, we don't have much more to cover. A few more items that are a little more complex and then you are all set with the knowledge of a millionaire," smiled Steve.

"Let's not put me in that category yet, Steve" Ryan chuckled as he got up off the couch and shook hands with Steve and headed towards the door.

"Have a great trip in the *happiest place on earth*," Ryan said.

"Thanks, we will. We love it there," responded Steve.

Ryan walked down the walkway towards the car and began thinking of how much he had learned so far this summer. When he got in the car, he grabbed his notebook and wrote down the day's lesson.

Time = Money The Longer You Hold a Property, The More Money You Make

Chapter 9
Partners

When Ryan woke up Friday morning, he was a little apprehensive about his meeting with Mel. Over the course of the past few weeks he had gained Steve's trust and felt confident in what messages Steve was conveying to him. However, besides the fact that Ryan got a B in Mr. Bodine's math class 11 years ago, he was not sure if he could trust the information he was going to provide would be accurate. The two things Ryan considered were first, Steve is partners with Mel on a few properties which was a good sign. Second, he was a teacher. Although he wasn't a real estate teacher, he must be trustworthy to be teaching in the school district so long.

On Friday mornings, Ryan didn't have any recreation programs scheduled. It was his one day to sleep a little later, as long as he was at the pizza shop by 11:00am.

He got in a little earlier to ensure that Mel didn't get there before he did. When Ryan got in, he dropped off his backpack in the back, clocked in, and went and took a seat in one of the booths. About two minutes later Mel walked in, notebook in hand.

"Hey Ryan, how's it going today?" Mel asked

"TGIF, Mel, TGIF (Thanks God It's Friday)," Ryan answered.

"What can I get you for lunch?"

Mel made his choice and Ryan placed their lunch order. Ryan was anxious to get started.

"How are things going at the school?" Ryan asked.

"No complaints. The kids change, and at times it is a little tougher than when you were there. But overall I still like having an impact on our youth, and I love the schedule. Home by 3:00 and off all summer!" Mel replied with a big grin on his face.

"Can't beat that," Ryan added.

"Are we ready to start?" Mel asked.

"Sure am."

"When I spoke to Steve, he asked me to cover two topics with you while he was gone. These are two very important topics but ones I think you will find very interesting and critical to your future success as a real estate investor. Those two topics are Partners and Tenants. For the sake of making it easy, let's do Partners today and Tenants next week." Mel said

"Sounds good to me," Ryan replied.

"Let me start by telling you that I have a partner in every property I own. I love having partners for many reasons, which we will touch on in a few minutes. Currently I have eight properties in my portfolio and have six partners in total. Some properties have one partner, some have two and on a few properties I have the same partner.

"As you obviously know, I am not a full time real estate investor. I have my job with the school but also invest in real estate on the side. This is the main reason I like dealing with partners so much,

"Partners are good for so many things when you are dealing in real estate part-time. The first and probably the most important reason is, it means less investment and less risk on your part.

"Obviously if you are looking at a house worth $100,000, you would normally have to put down 10%, or $10,000. But if you have a partner you only have to put down $5,000 each. It is much easier to come up with $5,000 then it is to come up with $10,000."

"That alone seems like a great reason to have a partner," Ryan answered in a strong tone.

"Yes and there are plenty more reasons. I will explain in a minute," responded Mel.

"It is also good if you are having trouble finding a property that will break even. The majority of time in some of the more expensive areas in the country, for a property to have positive cash flow, you need to look for multiple unit properties. These houses will obviously cost more money and a partner or two can help alleviate some of those costs. The property will still be positive, so it's still a good investment for everybody."

"I also like to have partners because it means that you split the responsibility of the property. Whether it is cut in half or in thirds depending on how many partners you have, it means you don't have to be married to the property 24 hours a day and do everything that comes up by yourself. Remember, although real estate is very profitable, there is still work that needs to get done. It could be repairs, deposits of rent checks, mailing of expenses, like mortgage payments, water, sewer, etc."

"Well, how do you go about finding a good partner?" asked Ryan.

"That is probably the hardest part of this process. A partner needs to be someone you trust and has the same goals as you do for the property. For example, if your partner wants to flip the property and you want to hold it for a long-term investment, you will encounter problems before you even get started. Partners at times can be family members and sometimes it can be friends but overall it must be someone you are comfortable with.

"The next thing I look for in finding a partner is someone that is good at things that I am not good at. For instance, I am good at finding the deal, structuring the deal, negotiating the deal and closing the deal. I also feel competent at working with the tenants and the whole rental process. However, when it comes to fixing a breaker or stopping a leak, my wife probably knows more than I do."

Ryan laughed and said, "me too, I wouldn't put myself up for handyman of the year."

"However, once you find a partner, it is critical that you sit down with them and prepare a professional operating agreement. You might think that everything is okay but there is going to be a time during the relationship that you will not always be in agreement. It doesn't take that long to create the document and it will save everyone hours of problems down the road. Some items that need to be included in the operating agreement are:

1.   What are the responsibilities of each partner (repairs, accounting, tenant relations)

2.   What are the goals of the property? (long term, short term)

3.   How will the voting on the property be handled? (majority or unanimous required)

4.   What if one of the partners passes away, does the property have to be sold?

5.   What if a partner wants to leave the property, how will that be handled?

"There are a few other items, but, this is the gist of it. If you don't have an operating agreement, you are really risking more than is necessary.

"Partners are also good for other areas that can help in your building of wealth. For instance, it is always good to hear different ideas and strategies. They might bring to light some things you didn't think about.

"Is that the two heads are better than one theory?" asked Ryan.

"Something like that," Mel replied.

"One of the other reasons I like using different partners is because it keeps me sharp on each particular property. If my buddy Dave calls me, he only wants to talk about the condo we have together in Florida. He doesn't really care about the other places I have. So in turn, I need to be on top of every detail on every property. I need to be able to talk intelligently on each one, so I do the work that is needed to ensure that I am up-to-date on each property."

"That makes sense." Ryan added. "Seems like partners are a good way to go," he added.

"I like it, but that also depends on each person's situation. If you are one who is a little controlling and always has to have things done your way, then a partnership might not be the best setup for you. However, as you can see there are also many advantages to having partners," Mel stated.

"I think that about wraps it up for today," said Mel. "How did I do? I have never taught anyone about real estate, only math."

"I think you did great. I really learned a lot today, and I can't wait for next Friday's meeting," answered Ryan.

"Okay, I'll see you next week, Ryan."

"Thanks again Mel. I really appreciate it." Ryan said as he walked over to pick up the delivery that was waiting for him on the counter.

Then Ryan got in his car grabbed his pen and wrote down the two lessons from the day's session.

Partners Mean Less Investment and Less Risk

Pick Partners That are Good at Things That You are Not

Chapter 10
Searching For A Good Tenant

Ryan's session with Mel was much more interesting then he thought it would be. Steve was definitely correct. Mel knew real estate and Ryan was glad he was willing to share his knowledge.

Ryan was getting to a point where he was starting to feel comfortable that he really knew what actions to take and what to look for when a buying property.

He thought one more session with Mel and maybe a few more with Steve and he would be ready to tackle the world. Steve was getting back from vacation on Saturday, but he and Ryan were not scheduled to meet until the following Friday night. That was fine because after this week's session with Mel, Ryan wanted to do a little more research and pick a place that he thought could be a good buying opportunity for his first deal.

It was now Friday morning and Ryan was heading over to the pizza shop to meet Mr. Bodine. This time when he arrived, Mel was already in the booth.

"Am I late?" Ryan asked.

"No you're not late, I tried to get here a little early because we might be going to a water park today in Wildwood," answered Mel.

"It's definitely hot enough for a water park today, that's for sure," added Ryan.

"As I mentioned last week, our topic this week is Tenants," Mel said.

"Over the course of your real estate career you are going to come across good tenants and bad tenants. However, there are many ways to do some prep work on potential tenants to ensure the good ones far out weigh the bad ones.

"I am sure Steve has already addressed the fact that you need to keep a professional relationship with your tenants and treat them like business partners. It is important that they know this is a business. Anytime you let them believe you are their friend, there is potential for them to try to take advantage of you.

"Rule #1. When reviewing potential tenants, never settle for a tenant you are not crazy about. What I mean by that is, just because the mortgage is due and you have not filled the apartment, it doesn't mean you should take someone you are not comfortable with. It is much harder to get someone out of the house once you put them in then it is to be smart and patient and try to find someone you believe is reliable. I realize that it might be a situation in which you could lose out on a month's rent, but in the long run getting the right tenant will pay off.

"The second step after you review potential tenants is to make sure you pull a credit report on every applicant you think is a strong candidate.

"There are many sites on the Internet you can use to pull this information for about $9.95. It is important to know your tenant's credit history to see if they will be able to pay the rent on a monthly basis. I can't tell you how many times I interviewed people that seemed honest and trusting, but then I pulled their credit report and found they had not paid multiple creditors in over five years!"

"How often does that happen?" asked Ryan.

"Let's just say not too often, but more than you think," answered Mel.

"Your pool of potential tenants depends on how much rent you are asking for. You might think you can get $1,000 a month for a two bedroom and that could be true, but if you lower that amount to $975 when advertising, you will get another 5-10 applicants to choose from. The good news about that is it heightens your chance to find a good tenant who is going to pay you on time and take care of your house. Plus, if you don't find a tenant you like after advertising at the $1,000 price, it will cost you another week of advertising in the paper which is usually more than the delta of a few months of that $25 extra dollars you were trying to get.

"Any question so far Ryan?" asked Mel.

"No, so far I am following right along," answered Ryan.

"Okay good, let's continue.

"Let's say that you have now decided on a tenant. It's now time to create the lease and prepare the paperwork to get that tenant in as quickly as possible. Here are some items I try to include in the lease.

"Try to negotiate with the renter a clause in the lease that he or she will take care of the outdoor maintenance such as the lawn care and snow removal. In most cases you will have to provide the shovel, rock salt, and lawn mower but it will save you about 20-30 hours a year if someone else handles that responsibility. Plus, it doesn't cost you anything if the tenant handles it. If they don't or can't because they are not fit for that type of labor, you will have to work out how you will handle it. You might need to hire a landscaper or do it yourself. However, if your rental property was a condo, the condo association would handle it.

"Other clauses I include are:

1) Always include an incentive clause in the lease. This clause states that if 12 consecutive payments are made on time, the tenant will be eligible for a bonus. You can pick whatever you want to give the tenant but we usually offer them a DVD/VCR player or a gift certificate. It's not too expensive and it is a small price to pay for 12 guaranteed payments a year. Plus, it's tax deductible and helps to give the tenant something to strive for.

2) If you are doing a multi-year lease, make sure you have built in yearly rent increases. Your taxes are bound to go up and it helps to be up-front with the tenants and make them aware far in advance. The one thing tenants don't like is surprises. If it is already documented, then everyone is aware of what will take place next year.

"Now that you are ready to have the tenant move in, there is one more thing I usually do. I give my tenant an information package to make it easier on them and at the same time ensure they are aware of everything regarding the property. Here is what I include in that information package:

1) Contact list of the name and phone number of the

landlord or property manager. (Never give them your home address or home phone number.) I also include the exact name that the checks should be addressed to and the address of where the checks should be sent.

2)   Twelve prepaid self addressed envelopes made out to the business address. This makes it easy for the tenant to just drop the check in the envelope and put it in a mailbox.

3)   Give them a utilities information sheet. This sheet should include the phone numbers of the gas and electric company, a cable company, and a phone company. The tenant will need to call these numbers to have the utilities switched over to their name and might need to occasionally call them for service problems.

"Now we have officially taken care of the tenant and they are all set to move in. There are a few other items I want to inform you of to protect yourself and keep everything organized.

"Although you might think you have great tenants in your house, you never know what they are going to say or do. Throughout the past two sessions we have talked about making sure you treat this like a business. One of the things you must do to ensure your protection is to make sure you move the property into the name of an LLC (Limited Liability Company). This will protect your assets in case an accident occurs on your property and you get sued. If the house is in an LLC, the worst possible case scenario is that you lose the property. If it is not in an LLC, the plaintiff has the ability to come after you for all your personal belongings including your own home.

"The next piece of protection is insurance. Everyone needs insurance on the house to close on the sale but make sure you are not taking a short cut on insurance. Have more than enough coverage on the house and additional liability coverage to help cover you in case of an accident on your property. Although insurance is something people don't think about everyday, it is relatively cheap for the safety it provides you."

"Wow this seems like a lot of stuff to remember," Ryan said

"It sounds like a lot but once you do it one time it will become second nature," responded Mel.

"The final thing we are going to talk about with regard to tenants and properties is organization.

"As your real estate portfolio continues to grow, organization will be more and more important. For each property I own, I create a summary on one page which has all the details of the property. For example, I include the mortgage company account number, the tenants' names and phone numbers and the realtor that sold me the house. I then keep one copy of this sheet at work and one at home. The reason these items are so important is because sometimes things come up on a particular property and you need to make a call to correct it. If you have all the information you need on one sheet, you will always have it with you in case of emergencies.

"I also usually bring a copy with me on vacation in case something pops up that cannot wait until I come home."

"I am usually pretty well organized, so I don't think I will have a problem with that part of the program," replied Ryan.

"Great, you are already ahead of the game," added Mel.

"Well, I think that about taps me out for information on my two topics Ryan," said Mel.

"I am sure it does," commented Ryan. "I can't thank you enough for spending time with me the last two weeks. I have learned so much about partners and tenants I feel like I am an expert," added Ryan.

"I am sure someday you will be an expert, but for now just take it slow and make sure you are always dotting your Is and crossing your Ts," responded Mel. "I have to run, I think even I could use a ride in the lazy river today," Mel said as he got up from the booth and headed for the door.

Once he walked out Ryan grabbed his notebook and wrote down the day's lesson.

Never Settle While Searching for a Good Tenant

Chapter 11
Tax Advantages In Real Estate

Almost a week had passed and Ryan was due to meet with Steve after Steve's two weeks vacation in Disney World. Over the past week, he thought a lot about some of the details Mel reviewed with him, and he had also spent some time getting more details about the condo complex he was looking at for his potential first investment. Ryan also kept his eyes peeled around the island for any new houses that went up for sale and hopefully ones in his price range.

By the time Friday came, he was ready for Steve. He had all his information on the condo, and he was also eager to tell him what he thought about Mel and the information he had provided him.

As usual for a Friday in late August, *Two Brothers Pizza* was busy and deliveries were piling up on the counter. Finally at 7:30, Brian and Jimmy took the phones off the hook because too many orders were coming in and they could not get the pizzas out in time. This rarely happens, but sometimes it has to be done. Otherwise, it would be impossible to fill all the orders.

Although Ryan was ready to meet Steve tonight, he didn't have too much time to think about it because he was so busy with deliveries. It was about 10:45pm when he was sitting by the TV in the pizza shop and heard Brian yell over, "Ryan, delivery for Steve Glass."

Ryan yelled back, "one minute, the Yanks have bases loaded two outs."

"Let me try this again. You have 30 seconds to pick up this delivery or it goes to someone else," Brian scoffed.

"Fine, I'll put it on in the car," Ryan answered.

During his ride to Steve's, the Yanks doubled off the wall with the bases loaded to take a three run lead in the 9th inning.

By the time Ryan pulled up to 600 Washington Drive, Steve's front door was open and just the screen door was closed.

He knocked softly, in case the kids were sleeping.

"Come on in Ryan," shouted Steve.

"Hey buddy, good to see you," Ryan answered. "How was your trip?"

"My trip was great. I love Disney World. Great customer service, the kids are smiling all day and you always leave there feeling like a kid at heart," answered Steve. "Did you miss me?"

"Well, I would be lying if I said I did. I must admit, although we missed two sessions while you were gone, Mel did a great job filling in for you and provided me with some great information on partners and tenants. I guess he really isn't "just a math teacher." Ryan said chuckling.

"I knew he would have good information for you. He's a smart guy who also invests part-time and got hooked on real estate right about the same time I did," Steve said.

"Did you bring any questions with you tonight?" asked Steve.

"Actually, I didn't because I thought we were at a point now where you might want to dictate what we should cover before the summer ends," responded Ryan. "Do you have any thoughts for Monday's lesson?"

"I am glad you asked. First, let me ask you a question. Is it okay if I bring someone to tennis with me on Monday?" asked Steve.

"I guess it's okay if they don't mind us talking about real estate while we play," responded Ryan.

"Actually, that's why I am bringing him. His name is Mark Mowbray. He's a friend of mine and a partner with me on a few houses we own. He is an accountant and I want him to explain to you the detail about some of the tax advantages of real estate and what you need to look for and track to ensure that you are maximizing your tax deductions. In the past we have spoken about the advantages of real estate in many forms, but we did not cover the tax advantages. Many people think this is the most important reason to invest in real estate."

"Is he the good golfer that lives on Bobby Jones Road, in the big house with the red door?" Ryan asked.

"Yes, that's him. Let me guess, you deliver to him?" Steve asked.

"Yes I do, and I have seen him multiple times put his clubs in his trunk while I am making other deliveries in that area. Plus one time when I knocked on his door, I saw him putting in his living room," answered Ryan.

"I don't think that will be a problem. Plus, the more people I can learn from the better," Ryan added.

"Okay, then. We'll see you on Monday morning," Steve said.

"You got it. I hope his backhand is better than yours," laughed Ryan as he walked back to his car.

Before Ryan met with Mel, he was a little nervous because he was not sure how comfortable he was going to feel asking him questions on what he knew with regard to real estate. After the first week, the two had built a good rapport, and Ryan felt very comfortable talking openly with Mel and asking him questions on topics he was not sure of.

However, he didn't feel nervous at all with Steve's other friend Mark. Maybe he was comfortable because Steve's last choice was easy to get along with and he assumed Mark would be also.

It was a hot Monday morning when Steve's car pulled up in the parking lot and he and Mark grabbed their rackets out of the back seat and headed over to the shack. Although Ryan was sweating from hitting some balls around with another customer, he grabbed his racket and met the men about 30 yards from the shack.

"What a scorcher!" exclaimed Steve as they shook hands.

"Yes it is," Ryan answered. "I heard it might hit triple digits today Steve."

"If it hits the triple digits today then it's time to shut it down, get in some air conditioning, and just relax and watch the Phillies," Steve said.

"Boy, I am getting sick of you talking about the Phillies all the time. I actually find them hard to watch," Ryan added. He then turned toward Mark and put out his hand to shake it.

"Good to see you again," Ryan said,

"Good to see you too," responded Mark.

"The good news today is that it shouldn't take you long to warm up Steve," Ryan joked.

"That's for sure," answered Steve.

"Mark, over the past two months I have been teaching Ryan about real estate and its benefits," Steve said.

"There certainly are enough of them, that's for sure," responded Mark.

"The only big topic we haven't hit on is the one that is your specialty, taxes and deductions," Steve added.

"Well, I am sure I can help. There are plenty of real estate tax advantages and I am more than happy sharing them with any of Steve's friends," responded Mark.

"Great!" Steve and Ryan said simultaneously.

"Okay, Mark, you have the floor. Could you explain to Ryan about some of the biggest tax advantages in real estate?" asked Steve, who was looking at Mark while still trying to stretch before tennis.

"Sure Steve, no problem. Ryan, let's start off with the biggest tax benefit, which is almost always the mortgage interest. Interest is tax deductible, which helps offset the income you are going to earn each month with the tenant's rent check. The reason I say it is usually the biggest deduction is because the first five to ten years of a mortgage, the interest each month is still between 90%-98% of your monthly payment. However, as you continue to hold the property, more and more payments get applied toward the principle which in turn lowers the overall yearly interest you are paying on the loan.

"Although the mortgage interest is usually the biggest deduction each year, there are still many more deductions that you can take as an owner.

"The best way to describe a deduction for the house is simple. Anything that costs you money for the rental property can be deducted. All items such as water bills, sewer bills, condo fees, property taxes, inspection costs, and repairs can all be deducted along with many more.

"There are some less obvious deductions you can take. These include a portion of your cell phone if you use it as a business line, a portion of your own personal mortgage if you use a room in the house as an office, and a mileage deduction for the miles traveled back and forth to the property," Mark added.

"What do you mean mileage?" asked Ryan.

"Well, the IRS allows you to deduct the mileage it takes for you to manage the property each year. Every time you go to a property, it could be to make a repair, pick up a rent check or just check on the property. You should add the number of miles it is round trip and note it for your expenses every time you go. Then at the end of the year, your accountant will take that mileage and multiple it by the allowable IRS deduction amount, which I believe was $.48 a mile the last time I checked," answered Mark

"Those are some nice tax benefits!" exclaimed Ryan.

"Yes they are, and that is one of the key reasons why we like real estate so much," answered Mark.

"However, there are a few more items I want to cover including depreciation and the 1031 exchange," added Mark

"Those sound complicated," Ryan said.

"They may sound complicated, but after you do it a few times they both will become your best friend in real estate investing from a tax perspective," responded Mark.

"Each year when you file your taxes there is the obvious deductions we have been speaking about. However, one deduction that helps on a yearly basis in offsetting some of the income from the rent, is depreciation. Depreciation is a deduction on the house at a pro-rated amount for the length of the mortgage. This varies based on the cost of the land, and the improvements on the land but it is definitely a real estate investors best friend.

"The reason this is important is because when you sell the house you will be subject to capital gains tax which is usually around 15%. However, the income you receive each year from the tenant's rent is taxed at the regular rate of income tax, which at times is double the capital gains rate. So depreciation reduces the amount of taxable income from the rent checks each year and changes that portion into a future capital gains tax that will be taxed when the property is sold."

"Oh boy, that makes sense but still sounds complicated," Ryan said with a puzzled look on his face.

"I know it sounds complicated but your accountant or tax specialist does this all the time so it is not a big deal for them to calculate it. The one thing you need to know is that this is a huge tax savings, almost 15% a year on the depreciation amount, which really adds up over time," responded Mark.

"That sounds good to me," added Ryan.

Mark looked over at Steve who just hit another ball out of bounds and said, "Steve, I never realized your backhand was so bad."

"I have been trying to say that nicely all summer," Ryan joked.

"Mark, I didn't bring you here today to talk about my backhand. Plus trust me, it has improved tremendously over the past two months," responded Steve.

"Okay, the final item I need to cover with you today is the 1031 exchange advantage. This is a real estate investor's best friend," Mark smiled.

"The 1031 tax exchange states, if you sell a property you can choose to defer the capital gains taxes if you take all the proceeds and invest them into another property.

"There are specific guidelines with regard to how long you have to invest the money in another property and who can hold the proceeds after your first sale prior to purchasing property number two.

"However, the reason the 1031 exchange is such a big advantage is because it gives you the ability to invest the money you would have to pay to the government on your previous sale. This then means you can afford a more expensive property, which would appreciate at a higher value. Let's break down one example for you.

"Let's say we bought a property for $100,000. After two years we sold it at $150,000. In using round numbers, we would be taxed on $50,000 profit (the long term capital gains tax is approximately $7,500). However, in a 1031 exchange we don't have to pay the $7,500 to the government now and we can use it in the next investment as additional down payment and pay the taxes on that down the road. Many real estate investors continue to roll this 1031 exchange over and over into the next property every time giving them more buying power.

"There are a few other specific guidelines that are included with a 1031 exchange. For example, you have to buy a property that is of equal or greater value then the original one purchased. You cannot touch any of the proceeds from the previous settlement, and you must buy a like for like property (rental for rental, business for business, etc).

"When it comes time for you to execute a 1031 exchange, there are plenty of web sites and information out there that can provide you specific details on the steps to follow to ensure you are not in conflict with the IRS tax guidelines. You are probably better off talking to a 1031 tax exchange specialist who can provide you the step by step process for your specific transaction.

"It's hard for a new investor to see how this benefits them so much right now, but as you continue to grow your portfolio you will see how the rolling of these profits back into larger and more expensive properties will help create larger appreciation and future profits."

"That does sound like a nice tax perk, that's for sure," answered Ryan. "Let's just hope I get to a point in my real estate career where

I am using the 1031 exchange flawlessly," added Ryan with a smile on his face.

"Oh, you'll get there," Steve said.

"I think we are almost out of time," Ryan said as he hit a passing shot by Steve for game point.

"Good, because I think I am all out of tax advantage topics," responded Mark as he walked to the back of the fence to get the ball that just passed Steve.

"Mark, I can't thank you enough for coming today and informing me on some of the tax benefits of real estate investing," Ryan claimed.

"Steve, I must say, you really have a knowledgeable group of friends, first Mel now Mark. You have really surrounded yourself with a plethora of real estate specialists," added Ryan.

"Plethora?" asked Steve. "I think it is time to go Mark. When Ryan starts pulling out college type vocabulary it must mean the heat is really getting to him," Steve grabbed his racket case and his water bottle and began walking toward the parking lot.

"I'll see you on Friday, Ryan," Steve yelled. "Next week will be our last session."

"Looking forward to it Steve. Thanks again Mark. It was good to see you again," yelled Ryan back over to the guys.

Ryan grabbed his notebook and wrote down this day's lesson.

Real Estate Provides Multiple Tax Advantages

Chapter 12
All Good Things Must Come To An End

Later that day, Ryan began to realize he only had one session left with Steve. He learned so much from Steve this summer and more importantly he learned what he wanted to do with his career and how he would approach it. Steve not only spent time explaining the benefits of real estate to Ryan but also gave him pin point examples to help him understand what strategies to put in place, what to look for, how to organize, and what areas need crisp attention to detail.

Ryan had been in school for a long time and had been in many classes, but he never learned as much as he did in the ten weeks spent with Steve this summer.

As it approached Labor Day weekend, the island started to quiet down. People started packing up for the summer and heading back home. Most of the vacationers that came to Beach, NJ, were headed back to Philadelphia, New York, and Connecticut. As much as Ryan liked the summer, the locals didn't mind it once the summer ended because everyone needed a break from the crowds, the traffic, and the overall craziness the town endured for those two plus months each summer.

It was another Friday night, the last one of the summer, and the pizza shop was still busy but not as busy as the past few weeks. After this weekend the deliveries would usually be cut in half and the drivers would go back to their regular shifts with two drivers on during the week and three on Friday night. In the *Two Brothers Pizza Shop,* the end of summer meant the peak season was over. It also meant that Brian and Jimmy could now take a vacation since both of them usually worked double shifts about 5 to 6 days a week to help cover the high demand with the increased population in July and August. As Ryan's shift began, he was watching some highlights on ESPN when Brian came out of the back with his apron on ready to start the night's shift.

"It's official. The Phillies are out of the race," Ryan said with a half smile on his face.

"Come on, you have to be a believer Ryan," Brian responded.

"Who could be a believer in a team that is 15 games back with 25 games left on the schedule?" Ryan answered.

"Talk to me when they are 15 back with 14 to play," Brian added.

"Expect that talk soon," Ryan laughed. "Hey, before we start today's shift I want to thank you for introducing me to Steve Glass. Today is our last meeting and I have learned so much from him over the course of the summer."

"No problem big guy, I'm here for you. However, when you make it big time, I want you to remember where you got your start," Brian joked.

"You got a deal!" Ryan answered.

That night the tips were pretty good, and the night moved along as expected. During the night Pop stopped by and had a few slices, and he and Ryan talked about the summer and the basketball league. They talked about what the team could have done differently and what areas Ryan needed to improve on for next year. They also analyzed the championship game about 10 different ways and spoke about what a shame it was they lost in the finals for the second year in a row. Just as Ryan walked Pop out the door, Brian yelled over, "Ryan, last one of the summer, 600 Washington Drive."

As Ryan had previously done all summer long, he grabbed the pizza and with a smile on his face, walked out to the car and headed down to the golf course area. Just like all good things that come to an end, so was his education about to end with Steve. The good news was he really found a mentor. Steve was someone Ryan trusted and someone he thought would help him if he needed guidance in the future. He also found a friend whom he admired and respected.

When Ryan pulled up to the house, all the lights were on. He walked up the walkway, knocked on the door and shouted, "Two Brothers Pizza".

"Come in Ryan," Steve yelled from upstairs.

"What's up pal?" Ryan asked

"Nothing much," Steve responded. "Ready for the summer to end?" Steve asked.

"Well, summer is a catch 22 situation. It is fun, busy and warm on the island, but I could use a break from the crowds like everyone else," Ryan answered.

"I will miss our meetings," he added.

"Me too!" exclaimed Steve. "How much for the pizza tonight?"

"This one is on me Steve. It is the least I can do for all your help and patience with me this summer," Ryan said

"You don't have to do that. I enjoyed it myself," Steve added.

"Well, it will make me feel better if you let me at least pay for one pizza," responded Ryan.

"Fine, one pizza and that's it," Steve said in a stern tone.

"What do we have in store for our final lesson?" asked Ryan.

"Not too much. I just want to bring up a few small items I think I forgot to mention over the summer, and then I want to hear about the condo complex you have been talking about," Steve said.

"Sounds good. I will be ready with bells on," Ryan responded.

Labor Day weekend is usually the second busiest weekend of the year. Everyone in town is getting ready for the last picnic of the summer, or their last big party or beach day before the summer ends on Monday. It was a busy weekend for Ryan also because it meant he had to work at the bar and grill on Saturday and Sunday night, which usually ended with him being exhausted on Monday.

When he woke up on the final Monday of the summer, he could not have asked for a better beginning. The sun beamed in through his blinds; it was going to be about seventy-eight degrees outside today, and he was headed for his final day at the tennis shack until next summer. As Ryan got out of the shower, he realized after today it was time for him to start his investing career. All the lessons he learned, all the notes he took, it was going to be time to put these words into action. Ryan grabbed his racket, his water bottle, and his notebook and headed to the tennis shack.

Ryan got to the tennis shack a few minutes before he usually started because he had to gather up some items to close the shack for the season. Just like all the recreation programs and activities in town, Labor Day marked the end of the summer there, too.

Right on schedule at 7:50 Steve pulled up in a mini-van.

"What is that?" Ryan asked

"I could not find my keys so I had to take my wife's car," Steve answered.

"Thank goodness you don't drive that around all day long. You would start being called the first ever Soccer Mom millionaire." Both men laughed.

"Let's get started, since I am sure you have a lot to do with the tennis shack closing down today," Steve said.

"As I mentioned the other night, I just want to cover some random topics I might have missed over the course of the summer that I think are critical to the success of a real estate investor.

"I am not sure if you currently use a budget, but if you don't it is a good idea to start using one. Budgets are great for home and for business because it helps you track where your money is going, especially in real estate. You need to have a budget for each property so you know how much you will need for repairs yearly, advertising costs if a tenant moves out, as well as other miscellaneous expenses that pop up during the year. A budget is also good to use at home because it shows you if you are spending more money than you want in a particular area. Maybe you didn't realize that you spent $450 on eating out last month or you spent $350 on golf two months ago. Not saying that you or anyone else can't spend that much on those items but maybe you really don't want to. Maybe you want to put more money away for your children's college education. At least you would know what areas need to be trimmed in order to accommodate that. Also make sure in your home budget you build in money for fun. A man or woman without fun is like a fish without water. Fun keeps the spirit strong and the body young.

"The next topic I wanted to review is all future real estate transactions," Steve said.

"Just when I thought I had you figured out, and I promised myself you would not lose me again, here we go. I think you lost me," responded Ryan.

"Hold on one second; once I explain you won't be lost," Steve added.

"It is important to treat each property and closing transaction like a separate business. That means you should have a separate bank account for each property and a separate binder for each property. You are going to come across condominium organizations and building inspectors for different towns that run their town or complex differently than others you own. You need to be prepared to cope with each one separately and prepare accordingly.

"The final item on my list for today is diversifying. In today's market and any other market there are always going to be ups and downs. For a year or two, condos could be hot, another year multiple families in a specific town might be popular. Sometimes specific areas grow in value at different times. For a few years the shore towns could be a hot investment. Another few years it could be commuter towns that show dramatic gains in value. It is important to stay as diverse as you can so you can ride the waves as other areas increase.

"If you have all your properties in one town and that town all of a sudden has a dramatic decrease in property values, your net worth and real estate portfolio will take a substantial hit. Now, it will definitely come back in time but while that area is coming back wouldn't you like to have another area that is growing by leaps and bounds?" Steve asked.

"Of course I would," Ryan replied.

"Exactly, so try to stay diverse in dwelling types and in locations," Steve added.

"Okay, now before we get going, I want to hear about this condo complex you have been researching," Steve said with a smile on his face.

"Well, it's a local one in town, called Harbor View, that I have been watching all summer long. I think they are affordable and I think it is an area that is undervalued. Beach, NJ is a shore town, and property has increased in value dramatically over the past 10 years, but these condos have not. I think people will need a place to live if they work in the casino. These are a perfect investment with some great up-side if they hit the same appreciation other properties in the town have seen.

"I also think a two bedroom is better than a one bedroom because it gives you the opportunity to get a small family in there and not just a couple or single man or women."

"Good thinking, Ryan. I am starting to think I taught you something this summer," Steve added.

"What prices are you looking at and did you run the numbers with the expenses?" asked Steve.

"Yes, I did run the numbers and I was happy with what I found. There are currently 4 two bedroom units for sale in a price range of $100,000-$110,000. For the sake of today's example let's say I am able to get one of them for $100,000. I would put 10% down and have a mortgage of $90,000. Then I calculated the expenses, which I broke down monthly as follows:

$205.00	Condo fee
$125.00	Taxes
$583.74	Mortgage
$29.58	Sewer, and yearly inspections.
$ 943.32	Total expenses per month

"One other side note. The condo fee for the complex includes: water, heat, insurance, garbage pick up, and outdoor maintenance," Ryan added.

"Sounds like you did some serious homework here," Steve commented. "Did you check what you think you could get for rent at these units?"

"I checked the local paper and there were 3 units for rent all asking between $975-$1,025. Let's say I get someone in there for $1,000 a month; the positive cash flow is +$56.68 a month!"

"Great!" Steve exclaimed.

"This sounds like an opportunity I would not pass up. Plus it also sounds like a great starter property with some good growth potential," Steve said.

"I must admit. I wasn't quite ready for you to spring all that information on me, good job!" added Steve.

"Well, I learned from the best!" exclaimed Ryan.

"I think that about wraps up our summer education Ryan. It has been a great experience for me and I want to thank you for being so attentive and eager to learn. It was a very rewarding experience for me, and I hope you got a lot out of it," Said Steve.

"It has also been a great experience for me. This summer has changed my life. I now know what I want to do, how I am going to do it and I have also made a new friend and mentor for life. Thanks again for everything," added Ryan.

"One thing before I go. I got you a graduation present."

"A graduation present? I should be the one buying you a present Steve," Ryan responded in a tone that was a little uncomfortable.

Steve reached into his tennis bag and gave Ryan a box about 5 inches long by about 2 inches wide.

"Go ahead open it," insisted Steve.

When Ryan opened the box there was a silver pen in it with an inscription that read "The Pizza Delivery Millionaire," Ryan just smiled and shook Steve's hand.

"Thanks again Steve."

"No problem. Just do me a favor. Use that pen every time you sign a new contract or closing papers on a new property. It is important to never forget where you came from. It defines who you are and how far you've come," Steve added.

"I will Steve, I can't wait to use it on my first deal," Ryan said with a smile on his face that reached from ear to ear.

As Steve walked back to his car Ryan opened the box again and looked at the pen in more detail. "The Pizza Delivery Millionaire." He liked that.

Review Of The 12 Lessons From The Book

1. Millionaires Can Look Like You and Me.

2. 90% of Millionaires Made Their Money in Real Estate.

3. In Real Estate, 10% Investment Buys You 100% of Product.

4. Tenants are What Make You a Millionaire in Real Estate.

5. Find Properties with Positive Cash Flow and You are On Your Way to Becoming a Millionaire.

6. To Be a Good Investor. It Helps to Be an Expert in the Area You Are Investing.

7. You Can't Spend What You Don't See. Forced Savings.

8. Time = Money. The Longer You Hold a Property, The More Money You Make.

9. Partners Mean Less Investment and Less Risk.

10. Pick Partners that are Good at Things that You are Not.

11. Never Settle When Searching for a Good Tenant.

12. Real Estate Provides Multiple Tax Advantages.

About The Author
Rick Vazquez

Rick Vazquez is currently a Business Operations Manger for International Business Machines Corporation, in Piscataway, New Jersey. Rick has over 20 years of business experience in dealing with customers, executives and business partners.

In 2003, Rick started investing in residential real estate part time, and has quickly built an impressive real estate investment portfolio. He has bought and sold over fourteen properties in that time frame totaling over $3.1 million dollars. He currently owns eight rental properties and continues to actively prospect for additional real estate assets to add to his portfolio.

Rick is a passionate individual who possesses a high energy level and enthusiasm in all aspects of his life. Whether writing, looking for properties, or driving IBM's business, Rick is constantly looking to create win/win situations for all parties involved.

Rick is a native of New Jersey, and when he isn't writing or working, he enjoys spending time with his loving wife and their two children Jordan and Ryan in their home in Central Jersey.

FREE BONUS
AUTHOR SECRETS
REVEALED

In this exclusive one on one interview with author Rick Vazquez, he goes into detail on the reasons for his success, tips on getting started and additional details on why real estate is such a great investment for everyone.

You can download this free recording at:

www.PizzaDeliveryMillionaire.com/freedownload.htm

To learn more about products and services based on

The Pizza Delivery Millionaire

Please visit our web site:

www.PizzaDeliveryMillionaire.com

or call: 866-PIZZA16 (749-9216)

<u>Our web site offers:</u>

*Pizza Delivery Millionaire start up investment package

*Pizza Delivery Millionaire Logo Merchandise

*Details on Speaking Engagements and Book Signings

Printed in the USA
CPSIA information can be obtained
at www.ICGtesting.com
JSHW082212140824
68134JS00014B/586